HOW GOOD IS YOUR GRAMMAR?

HOW GOOD
IS YOUR
GRAMMAR?

100 quiz questions – the ultimate
test to bring you up to scratch

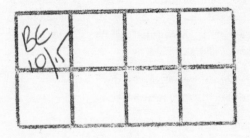

John Sutherland

First published in 2015 by Short Books
Unit 316, Screenworks
22 Highbury Grove
London N5 2ER

10 9 8 7 6 5 4 3 2 1

A CIP catalogue record for this book is
available from the British Library.

ISBN 978-1-78072-257-3

Printed and bound in Great Britain by
CPI Group (UK) Ltd, Croydon, CR0 4YY

Illustration on cover and p.177 © Honor C. Appleton /
Mary Evans Picture Library
Cover design by Andrew Smith

For Randolph Quirk

'Keep it Simple.'
– Dying words of Bill W, Founder of AA

'I am almost sure by witness of my ear, but cannot be positive, for I know grammar by ear only, not by note, not by the rules. A generation ago I knew the rules – knew them by heart, word for word, though not their meanings – and I still know one of them: the one which says – but never mind, it will come back to me presently.'
– The Autobiography of Mark Twain, 1924

'I couldn't possibly have sex with someone with such a slender grasp on grammar.'
– Russell Brand

Contents

Preface: 'Bring Back the Grammar!'

I had my early education at a grammar school (founded, as we were daily reminded, in the reign of Henry VIII). So did Shakespeare. I like to think of that shared heritage between me and the Bard whenever I reflect on how those Etonians, whose alma mater teaches much more important things in life than grammar, are taking over the world.

The Germans call their equivalent institutions '*gymnasiums*', the French, '*lycées*' (from the Latin '*lyceum*', a hall for lectures). These names tell us a lot about those countries. As does the epithet 'grammar' about ours. And – unloveliest word – 'comprehensivisation'. The abolition of the 'grammar' school, in the 1960s, and with it the 'eleven plus', has coincided with a general relaxation of the nation's care about grammatical correctness. Decline or linguistic democracy?

One of our political parties (the one most pervaded with Etonism, as it happens) has pledged to 'bring back the grammar'. Tory grammarians see 'good English' as no less necessary a defence of the nation than Trident submarines. Their hearts warm at the mention of the title of the Fowler brothers' book *The King's English* (1906), and Kingsley Amis's homage–treatise of the same name (1997). Flying the same banner is 'zero tolerant' Lynne Truss with her delightful defence of punctuational rectitude, *Eats, Shoots & Leaves*.

Opposing them are the grammatical *sans-culottes* – rebels, anarchists and *Guardian* readers all – who see even the extreme alternative (so-called 'wankers' grammar') as a refreshing *non serviam* (or 'up yours!', as the wanker would say). Grammar is, nowadays, hot politics.

I'm no linguist, although for several years I headed a distinguished department of 'Language and Literature'. It was that way round. Language precedes use of language.

It was, for me, a happy neighbourhood. I liked the common sense that my 'language' colleagues brought to bear on that human skill which, above all else, makes us human – our way with words, and their ways with us.

The Survey of English Usage, founded by Randolph

Quirk, has for six decades surveyed, with a tolerantly clinical eye and ear, how we actually use language. The unit has published, under its present director, Professor Bas Aarts, an app – *the interactive Grammar of English* – for tablets and smartphones.[1] It is crystalline in its clarity and avoidance of jargon – but entirely without prescription or moral judgment (i.e. 'good grammar' versus 'bad grammar'). There are only two imperatives it implicitly enjoins. That the language we use should make sense, and that the sense made should be appropriate to the situation. That's it. Oh, and it helps a bit if you know how it works.

Situation is the more interesting to me. I love the way grammar flows like liquid to adapt to its situation, as it does, pre-eminently, in poetry. Or it can be clunkily pedantic, as in legal discourse (e.g. Groucho's 'party of the first party shall hereafter be known as the party of the first party...'). The poet's discourse reveres the richness of ambiguity and the erotics of vague. The lawyer's discourse labours to disambiguate.

What follows is not a grammar rule book nor what used to be called a 'primer'. It is a set of ruminations by someone who has worked with words and who, like M. Jourdain with his prose, has discovered he has been using grammar all his life – more or less right(ly). And who relishes its curiosities.

---

1   http://www.ucl.ac.uk/english-usage/apps/ige/

TEST ONE

Each of the following 25 questions revolves around a grammatical error: real, alleged, disputable or simply fun to think about. Answers are at the end of the section. Keep your score.

1   Picture two university-educated young men. **'This is I, Hamlet the Dane!'** shouts one. **'It ain't me, babe,'** croons the other. Which of them is using the personal pronoun (I, me) correctly?

2   **'Different to'; 'different from'; 'different than'**. Which is correct?

3   In his entertaining disquisition, *English for the Natives: Discover the Grammar You Don't Know You Know*, Harry Ritchie defiantly decrees: **'It is not wrong to say disinterested instead of uninterested.'** Is he right?

4   In his anti-stickler polemic *AccidenceWill Happen* (charming title), Oliver Kamm asserts that the **'flat adverb'** is quite permissible – in the face of generations of schoolteachers, who have outlawed it. What's a flat adverb?

5   One can say **'a book well worth the read'**, and **'a path well worth the walk'**. Why can't one say **'a meal well worth the eat'**?

6   ***Bill and Ted's Excellent Adventure*** is a cult movie. But why not 'Bill's and Ted's Excellent Adventure', and in what circumstances would the extra apostrophe be correct?

7   **'Frankly, my dear, I don't give a damn'** has been voted the number one movie line of all time. What's the little *lapsus grammaticae*?

8   Why keep **'elder'** around when **'older'** (e.g. 'older brother', 'elder brother') works as well?

9   According to Kingsley Amis, **'The reason he smashed the car is because he was drunk'** (interesting Amisian sub-narrative embedded here) is the kind of mistake perpetrated by 'well-meaning illiterates'. Why?

10   *The Sun Also Rises*. According to Fowler, the word **'also'** is an **adverb**, not a **conjunction**. How should one observe the rule? Does Hemingway?

11   **'The Californian Poppy is the state flower'**; **'The California Poppy is the state flower'**. Both statements are horticulturally true, and Google throws up both. But one is ungrammatical. Which? And why?

12   What is the grammatical error in the following, from the most famous work of literature in English? **''Tis given out that, sleeping in my orchard / A serpent stung me'**?

13   In September 2014 *Scientific American* published an article entitled **'Diversity in Science: Where are the Data?'**. Should it be **'is the Data'**?

14   Why do grammar-fearing Scots use **'amn't I'**, not **'aren't I'**?

15   On 16 March 2015, the *Guardian* printed in its 'Corrections and Clarifications' column: **'Grammar Corner: We used "dependent",**

the adjective, where we should have used "dependant", the noun, in two articles in Monday's paper.' Is this a distinction worth making?

16 'If the pedestrian has already stepped into the road they are assumed to have right of way' (*Highway Code*). Singular subject, plural verb, ungrammatical?

17 'Telephone' / 'Television'. Which of the two, for purists, is ungrammatical, and why?

18 Spot (you'll be the zillionth to do so) the error in the following overture statement at the head of every instalment of the TV series *Star Trek*: 'Space – *blah, blah, blah –* / To seek out new life and new civilisations / To boldly go where no man has gone before.'

19 *Less Than Zero*. What's ungrammatical in the title of Bret Easton Ellis's bestselling novel?

20 'I will die, and nobody shall save me!!' What the luckless Frenchman shouts as he drowns at the British seaside (this, incidentally, is an old grammatical chestnut). No one on the beach

makes a move to save their fellow European. Why not?

21 What's ungrammatical, if anything, about the title of this Judy Garland song: **'The Man That Got Away'**?

22 **'If I was a rich man / Ya ba dibba...'** It's a frequent misquote. **'If I were...'** is correct. What is subjunctivitis (as it's been called) and why does it matter – if indeed it do?

23 A short witty letter, in the *Guardian*, 24 April 2015, reads: 'Driving to the Bluewater shopping centre, from the A2, I'm always puzzled by the instruction to **"Use Both Lanes"**.' What, grammatically, should the road sign say?

24 What's wrong with the following sentence: **'I'd like to go either to Oxford, or Cambridge or – failing all else – Leicester University'**?

25 **'When I, John Sutherland, went to Leicester University, I had to decide whether I wanted to be a student of literature or a historian.'** True – but what's the *lapsus grammaticae*?

Solutions to questions 1–25

1. 'This is I, Hamlet the Dane!'; 'It ain't me, babe'. Which is using the personal pronoun correctly?

Both of them are. Strictly the verb 'to be' takes the nominative pronoun ('I', in Hamlet's case). The demotic verb 'ain't' means 'is not' (e.g. 'is you is, or is you ain't my baby?'). But 'ain't', for reasons of its own, takes the object pronoun ('me', in Dylan's case). Horses for courses, as ever in things grammatical.

2. 'Different to'; 'different from'; 'different than'?

The iron schoolroom rule used to be always 'from', because of the Latin parentage of the prefix '*de/di*'. Catherine Soanes, in the *Oxford Words* blog, commonsensically decrees 'different to' and 'different from' don't have any difference from each other, or to each other, and notes that 'than' (which grates on British ears) is more common in America. But Anglophile F. Scott Fitzgerald would never have said to Hemingway that the rich 'are different than you and me'. Other grammarians point out that 'than' is comparative (e.g. 'Hemingway was taller than Fitzgerald') and 'different' implies something contrastive – hence 'to' or 'from' are the best choices.

3. Harry Ritchie decrees: 'It is not wrong to say disinterested instead of uninterested.' Is he correct?

If Harry Ritchie found himself in court (heaven forbid) would he want a 'disinterested' (i.e. impartial) judge or an 'uninterested' judge (one not listening and doing a crossword under his bench)?

4. What's a 'flat adverb'?

'Quick' and 'wrong' are 'flat adverbs' – i.e. they have the same form when used adverbially as they do when treated as an adjective. For example 'Vin Diesel stars in *Fast and Furious*, where he drives fast and furiously'. 'Fast' is flat. 'Fastly' would be absurd and, if we credit Kamm, 'he drives fast and furious' is OK too. 'Flat', oddly, can itself be a flat adverb: 'His voice is flat – he sang flat.'

5. Why can't one say 'a meal well worth the eat'?

The infinitive, in English, can sometimes become a noun (with 'to' changed to 'the'), but there's no rule controlling it that I know of. In German, the practice is universal: e.g. '*auch das Essen wert*' (well worth the eat) is quite respectable. Well worth the consider (and yes, that's OK in German as well – '*das Betrachten wert*').

6. Why not 'Bill's and Ted's Excellent Adventure'?

Michael Adams explains it elegantly on his *Oxford Words* blog: 'Bill and Ted... knew that when you have a "compound possession" – that is, when something belongs to two people at the same time – you only need one apostrophe. Thus, it's not "Bill's and Ted's Excellent Adventure." Only Ted's name carries the possessive.' Had the duo gone on different trips through time, in different phone boxes, two possessives in the title would have been quite in order. Good to know that a third film of the bodacious couple's adventures, 30 years on, is planned.

7. 'Frankly, my dear, I don't give a damn.' What's the little *lapsus grammaticae*?

'Frankly', placed where it is at the head of Rhett Butler's sentence, is an 'attitude adverb' (of which another, much despised example is 'hopefully'). He doesn't mean he's speaking 'frankly' (i.e. using 'damn' rather than 'darn' in a lady's presence). The sentence compresses something along the lines of 'To be absolutely frank with you, Scarlett, I don't give a damn about you any more, to use rather too frank a term'. But who gives a damn?

8. Why keep 'elder' when 'older' works as well?

Better even. Who says 'how eld is your brother?' Our resident Middle-English-Man is glad to see his old (eld, ald, auld) monosyllable still in current circulation. It has a good claim to survival. Dignity. What *puissance* would be lost if our aldermen were titled 'oldermen'. Church elders would not like being called 'dog-collared wrinklies', nor would we look up to them as reverently if they were. 'Elder son', in a legal system where primogeniture still rules, has a useful punch to it. Live on, old word. And, as Harry Ritchie points out – buildings can be 'old', but not 'elderly'. The old (elder) word humanises.

9. Is 'The reason he smashed the car is because he was drunk' the kind of mistake perpetrated by 'well-meaning illiterates'?

It should be, according to the King's and Kingsley's grammar, 'He smashed the car because he was drunk'. The phrase 'the reason is...' dilutes: like adding too much water to your whisky. *Hic!*

10. *The Sun Also Rises*. 'Also' is an adverb, not a conjunction. How should one observe the rule? Does Hemingway?

Yes and no. It depends how you read Hemingway's

title. If along the lines of 'The moon, also the sun, rise every 24 hours', it's a conjunction ('also' could be replaced by 'and' without loss of meaning). In 'The sun goes down daily but it also rises daily' it's adverbial. It's interesting that the title of the Spanish translation of this novel (set in Spain) is *Siempre sale el sol* – 'always rises the sun', which is, surely, purely adverbial. Nowadays the rule is generally relaxed, and 'also' is routinely described as a 'conjunctive adverb', which smooths over my uncertainty and flattens the Fowlerian objection.

11. 'The Californian Poppy is the state flower'; 'The California Poppy is the state flower'. Which statement is ungrammatical? And why?

'California Poppy' is correct. But it is not, as it may first seem, because the word 'California' is an adjective. As Bas Aarts explains, '"California" in "California poppy" is not an adjective. Although it appears before a noun, as adjectives often do, this is a proper noun modifying another noun (another example: "London taxi").' 'Californian' commonly means 'resident of the state', as in 'a California tax return must be filled out by all wage-earning Californians'. It's the same with all 50 states. Sometimes oddly. Residents of Utah are called 'Utahns', which is rarely heard outside the state, evoking as it does the image of something which ought to be behind bars in a zoo.

12. ''Tis given out that, sleeping in my orchard / A serpent stung me'? What is the grammatical error?

At last, the famed dangling participle. Is the serpent sleeping, or is Hamlet's father sleeping? Or are both in the land of nod? A herpetologist mildly objects that there are few fatally venomous snakes around in Denmark, in the deep of winter – which, the first lines of the play inform us, is where the action is, seasonally. But who cares about such piffling probabilities when a participle is dangling? There is, indeed, something rotten in the state of Denmark.

13. 'Diversity in Science: Where are the Data?'. Should it be 'is the Data'?

We're tiptoeing through a grammatical minefield. 'Data' is the plural of the Latin '*datum*' – item of information. But over time 'data' has taken on the character of a 'mass noun'. The voluminous documentation around the Data Protection Act treats the word it's all about as singular. In science it's trickier, because a single 'datum' can controvert a host of other data. The magazine can be comfortable with its plurality, even if it disconcerts the ear. There's a lot of blur around Latin neuter plural loan words in English. Every committee meeting, for example, will have an 'agenda'. But no one asks, looking around for the vital piece of paper, 'Where are the agenda?' or 'Madam chair, may I draw your attention to agendum 5?'. 'Media' swings both ways, singular or plural, depending on context, but is more often plural (except when it's a bunch of table-tapping mediums). Addendum and stadium pluralise as addendums and stadiums. 'Bacteria' is an interesting case. The singular 'bacterium' is used not for individual critters (they're never solitary) but for small groups of them. Our resident Roman is bemused.

14. Why do Scots use 'amn't I', not 'aren't I'?

Because it's correct, you Sassenach eejit! You wouldn't say 'I are', would you? Why then say 'aren't I'?

15. 'Dependent', the adjective, versus 'dependant', the noun. Is this a distinction worth making?

No – unless you want to stress the fact that you're a stickler for grammatical correctness, however pifflingissimo. Or, more likely, the paper's witty style editor, David Marsh, is having some in-house fun about the *Grauniad*'s venerable history of misspelling. There's no risk to meaning whichever spelling is used. I personally don't see any point in preserving the distinction, nor does the IRS, the American tax authority (who wants to tangle with them?), which asks those filing their returns if they have any 'dependents'. Britain's HMRC still goes, crustily, for 'dependants'. Harumph.

16. Singular subject, plural verb, ungrammatical?

If you don't know the sex of the hypothetical pedestrian 'they' is locally acceptable – awful as it sounds. The alternative 's/he' is trendy but barbaric – and you can type it but you can't 'say' it. If you spell it out, 'he or she' creates gender precedence, and 'she or he' has an overtone of Jack Horner's 'what a good boy am I'.

17. 'Telephone' / 'Television'. Which of the two, for purists, is ungrammatical, and why?

The first is grammatically correct, the second incorrect. Telephone is from the Ancient Greek τῆλε (*tệle*, 'afar') + φωνή (*phōnê*, 'voice, sound'). Television has the same Greek prefix but it's conjoined with the Latin '*visio*', meaning 'sight'. It's 'mongrelised'. The English language, like Crufts, has strict breeding rules – particularly with loan words. The editor of the *Manchester Guardian*, C. P. Scott, said, in 1926, when the term for the new technology was announced: 'Television? The word is half Greek and half Latin. No good will come of it.' Perhaps, looking at current schedules, he had a point.

18. Spot the error: 'To seek out new life and new civilisations / To boldly go where no man has gone before.'

And, of course, to boldly split infinitives – a hoary prohibition, but still, forlornly, invoked. It's the result of the chronically floating nature of 'to' (technically known as 'the infinitival particle') and its routine attachment to verbs. Other languages don't have the problem: e.g. 'To be, or not to be', '*être, ou pas être*', '*sein, oder nicht sein*'. More offensive nowadays than any fractured infinitive, is 'no man'. It should be 'no one', unless one thinks Uhuru invisible. But, what the hell, space is man's ('real' man's) last frontier.

19. *Less Than Zero*. What's ungrammatical?

Since 'zero' is numerical it should, pedantically, be 'Fewer Than Zero'. 'Less' is usually spatial, or used when referring to uncountable mass nouns; as in 'there's less room for my luggage in this rack than I thought; I should have brought fewer bags' – the room for luggage is not described in discrete, countable units, the number of bags is. If Ellis had used a determiner, not a numerical, as in 'Less Than nothing', it would have been grammatically inoffensive. But it's literature – who's complaining?

20. 'I will die, and nobody shall save me!!' Why does no one save their fellow European?

It's not xenophobia, but death by bad grammar. Both 'will' and 'shall' are predictive verbs. They forecast. But 'will' carries, etymologically, a stronger overtone of 'want', or 'wish to'; 'shall', in certain contexts, carries an overtone of stern prohibition – 'you shall not do this'. Hence the misapprehension: 'I want to drown, and nobody is permitted to help me.' *Adieu, mon brave*.

21. What's ungrammatical, if anything, about 'The Man That Got Away'?

Welcome to the 'that / who' minefield. It's a fairly straightforward distinction, in everyday discourse. The relative pronoun 'that' goes with objects and things, 'who' with people. Worth retaining as a rule of thumb. Such examples can often be defended on grounds of local necessity, even if they are strictly solecisms. It's easier, for example, for Garland to hold the vowel open with 'thaaaaaaat' than it is with 'whoooo', which would make her sound more owl than diva.

22. 'If I was a rich man / Ya ba dibba' should be 'If I were…' Why does it matter?

'Damn the subjunctive,' said Mark Twain, 'it brings all our writers to shame.' He was referring to a grammatical mood, in which the verb is adapted from its normal usage to express something that isn't, in fact, the case – such as something hoped for, expected, possible etc. Its constant misuse was what so infuriated Twain. It's drifting into disuse, but still has some utility where the 'if' hypothecates something wholly impossible – as it does in the *Fiddler on the Roof* ditty, where the traditionally plural form 'were' should be used, despite referring to the prospects of the first person singular. In his blog, Bas Aarts has an informative entry on the subjunctive and the interesting fact that it is alive and well in pockets of England and the US.[2]

23. 'Use Both Lanes': what, grammatically, should the road sign say?

Not 'Use Either Lane', because that would imply you could overtake on either side, thereby transgressing the rule of the (British, not American) road. 'Both' must, unfortunately, stand and continue to puzzle. America has a blunter way

2 https://grammarianism.wordpress.com/2015/05/21/ does-english-have-a-subjunctive/

with highway signage and would simply instruct: 'Two Lanes'. My favourite US traffic sign is the one on the I-10, the Santa Monica Freeway: 'Thru Traffic OK'.

24. What's wrong with the following sentence: 'I'd like to go to either Oxford, or Cambridge or – failing all else – Leicester University'?

'Either / or' is strictly dualistic. Alternative ('this or that') only. There can't be three or more, any more than there can be three alternatives. I, by the way, went to Leicester University. Oxbridge, for good reasons, doubtless, declined my application with them. Or should that be 'with it'?

25. 'When I went to Leicester University, I had to decide whether I wanted to be a student of literature or a historian.' What's the *lapsus grammaticae*?

Let pedantry be unconfined. Because the stress falls on the second syllable ('histORian') the 'h' is phonetically downgraded and unaspirated. Therefore 'an historian' is correct, as in 'an hour'. In 'hospital', by contrast, the stress is on the first syllable ('HOSpital'), and 'a hospital' is correspondingly correct. Got it? Good. Forget it.

What's your score?

If you racked up fifteen or more correct(ish) answers well done, you. You're sound as a nut, grammatically. But there is a more important reward for you than smugness. Knowing good grammar means you are free to boldly use bad grammar. It's a privilege worth having, ain't it? But first, some background on the rules you might be looking to break, followed by a few no-nos and some reforms I'd make if I were master of the grammatical universe.

There will be questions throughout – answers at the end of each section.

RULES: WHO NEEDS THEM?

*R*ules presume rule givers – an authority. Rulers. 'Ring givers', as the Anglo-Saxons called them. Who, or what, rules today? In their Edwardian bible of grammar (1906), the Fowler brothers had no doubt. 'Edwardian' meant literally that: *The King's English*. Edward VII's kingo-lingo. Just like the coins with his head on the obverse, and the postage stamps whose backside his subjects faithfully licked.

> **26** 'Obverse' and 'reverse' – what's the difference? And, while we're at it, 'opposed' and 'diametrically opposed'?

A language, it's said, is a dialect with an army behind it and an empire giving it sovereignty. Britannia's Royal Navy once ruled the waves and, as the 20th century dawned, had secured the largest empire, and linguistic domain, since Rome's.

However, the 20th century was destined, historically and dialectally, to become America's. The British Empire, over which the King's English ruled, would shrink to a couple of barren islands and surly Ulster — whose dialect the Fowlers would have regarded as no more worthy than the clucking of chickens.

The Fowlers did fight against this onward march of American English: 'Americanisms', they decreed, should, when they were unavoidable, be placed between inverted commas. Given that American phraseology has become so entirely pervasive today, we might wonder what such a regulation would mean for modern punctuation: '"Man", I'm "all over it", believe me, "no problemo".' Call it the disinfectant quotation mark. *Procul, O procul este, profani.*

---

27   Two people, one American, one British, are asked, 'Are you happy?' Each replies, 'Quite.' What different meaning might one reasonably deduce from their identical answers?

So, with the rise of the US and the decline of the old empire, the notion of Fowlerian national discipline has shrunk and withered. The last hold-out — the home of received pronunciation and correct grammar – was the BBC. Over the first half of the 20th century it held firm in the face of international change and imposed a kind of 'flat iron' on the national tongue, regularising how speech should be spoken.

> **28**   Is *Have I Got News for You* – the title of the long-running BBC quiz show – a question? If not, what is it?

During this time, as with pronunciation, grammar was a 'received' thing – via the radio receiver.

Of course, that sense of sovereignty no longer exists. Authority has been diffused and erased. But, as with its four (American) Trident submarines, Britain still clings on to rule-governed 'English'. It signals world power. Nostalgically.

Solutions to questions 26–28

26. 'Obverse' and 'reverse'; 'Opposed' and 'diametrically opposed' – what's the difference?

They are differences worth knowing. The first two are used to describe the two faces of a coin.

Philip Larkin nails it, rather uncheerfully, in his poem, 'Many Famous Feet have Trod': 'This old discoloured copper coin is death / Turn it about; it is impenetrable / Reverse and obverse.' One face is the obverse and the other face is the reverse. The Queen's head, on English coins, is always obversive. Somehow that sounds disrespectful. As for 'opposed' and 'diametrically opposed', there is no significant difference. Think of a circle. At any point on its radius there is a single point, on the other side, which is farthest away. It would be more exact to say 'diametrically separate'.

27. 'Quite': British versus American.

The adverbial modifier 'quite' is as slippery as a wet bar of soap. As someone who's lived in both countries, I've found British-English speakers tend to mean 'somewhat, a little bit, not much'. American-English speakers, by contrast, tend to mean 'entirely, wholly'.

28. *Have I Got New for You*. Is that a question?

As posed it's a rhetorical question (i.e. one that doesn't require an answer). An exclamation mark and the addition of the determiner / quantifier 'some' and a deflating vocative would help, e.g. 'Do I have some news for you, my little green Martian friend! Listen up!' But I suspect that any precise description of what is going on here would be like the fabled winky-wanky bird. It would go round in ever-decreasing circles until it disappeared up itself in ultimate piffledom.

WE NEED RULES

*I*n the larger, human sense, we need rules, wherever they originate and whatever they do for us. It's a species thing.

One humble item of everyday life, loud but never sounded, will make the point. The life-jacket whistle. We are all pedantically instructed how to use it in the lesson that is sermonically delivered on take-off ('in the unlikely event of our landing on water') to the belted airline passengers.

Safety belts have certainly saved lives. But not a single passenger in the history of civil aviation, I would guess, has been saved by that whistle. They might as well give the passengers kazoos or party poppers. But it means something. The crew's instruction enforces symbolic collective obedience, during the flight, to the captain's will ('aye aye, skipper').

That obedience is what saved 155 passengers (none perished) in the most dramatically filmed emergency landing on water in recent history. On 15 January 2009, having crash-landed safely on the freezing Hudson River, Captain Sully Sullenberger instructed everyone on board to exit onto the plane's wings, life-jackets inflated (but only when safely outside the craft – remember the lesson). 'They all did what they were told,' he said. Sully, like the captains of old, stayed in the plane until everyone was evacuated.

Those 155 saved souls should all have got out their little whistles and given a fanfare of honour to the man who saved their lives. But they also owed their lives, in a larger sense, to obedience to rule – symbolised by that very whistle on their life vests. Living by the rule saved their lives.

This story also demonstrates how Sully Sullenberger's profession is one in which high proficiency in English grammar is a no-question-about-it must-have. Grammatical English is the *lingua franca* (misnamed) of international air control.

'This are your captain speak, ladies and gentlemans. We shall be flieging at 39,000 foots. Tin whores in all flutime.'

The International Civil Aviation Authority has a rating scale for linguistic competence in English. There are six fields:

1. Pronunciation
2. Structure
3. Vocabulary
4. Fluency
5. Comprehension
6. Interaction

The second, 'Structure', focuses specifically on grammar. Proficiency in this field is measured on a scale of one to six:

1. Expert
2. Extended
3. Operational
4. Pre-operational
5. Elementary
6. Pre-elementary

The definition for 'Expert' grammatical competence is: 'Both basic and complex grammatical structures and sentence patterns are consistently well controlled.' 'Elementary' is: 'Shows only limited control of a few simple memorised grammatical structures and sentence patterns.'

'Enjoy flieg yours, Ladies and Gentlemans. And thank you for flying Final Destination Airlines.'

Rules create an ethos of order, a framework, even if, like the life-jacket whistle, they're never taken out and tootled. More honoured in the breach than the observance, as Hamlet says (Shakespeare, of course, merrily marched his language through that breach).

---

29   A social rules question. When should one use 'Madam', 'Madame' and 'Ma'am'?

Linguistic rules and grammar create a rule-governed environment. The rules may in themselves be pointless or petty (no double negatives, no sentences ending in a preposition, no split infinitives, etc). But human beings, social animals that we are, need authority, even *in extremis*. Primo Levi records that the filthy concentration camp ablutions had signs reading 'Now Wash your Hands'.

---

30   How can a single sentence containing the words 'ate', 'often', 'waistcoat' and 'golf' tell us someone's social class?

The strenuousness with which the rules are imposed is a historically variable thing. The anthropologist Mary Douglas notes that draconian insistence on, in themselves footling, rules is an index of social nervousness. It's safe to say we're in an acutely nervous phase at the moment. 'Sticks and stones may break our bones,' says the old proverb, 'but words will never hurt us.' We certainly think they can hurt us. Hence 'PC' muzzling.

> 31   'Waitress', under feminist pressure, is a no-no, as is the Scottish 'clerkess'. Does that mean 'princess' should go as well? Will the Court Circular of the future announce 'the Prince and Prince of Wales spent Christmas at Balmoral'?

If the English people have an ideology, it is 'pragmatism' – play it as it lays ('lies'? let's be pragmatic and grant that rhyme can sometimes take precedence over grammar). In 1712 Jonathan Swift (the purest prose practitioner our language has, George Orwell thought) was in utter despair about the State of English. He wrote a proposal for the establishment of an institution of linguistic control, such as the French, with their Académie Française, had had laying down linguistic law for 80 years. Its aim would be 'to ascertain and fix our Language for ever'. That fixity, thank God, has never happened. The liquid unfixity of English, as spoken and written, is one of its strengths and glories.

Solutions to questions 29–31

29. Social rules: when should one use 'Madam', 'Madame' and 'Ma'am'?

Etiquette sets grammatical tank-traps for those not aware of the (specifically) English class system. Why, for example, is it 'Ladies' Day' at the Wimbledon tennis finals but 'England's women footballers' in their World Cup competition? (And why not 'World's Cup'?) You still see toilet doors with 'Ladies' and 'Gents' on them; so where do the 'sluts' and 'low-lifes' relieve their naughty bladders? These toilet labels have, over recent years, gone semiotic – the words themselves hold no specific connotation, and represent nothing more than the stick-figure logos widely used in their place. But, strangely, the male stick figure often has his legs closed and the female stick figure has hers open. Go figure. The etiquette surrounding the use of 'Madam', 'Madame' and 'Ma'am' is no less perilously balanced. French waiters unerringly identify, and respectfully address, *femmes* of a certain age as '*Madame*', not '*Mademoiselle*'. Madam (from the French, 'my lady') is polite, although tainted by brothel-keeping connotations. Ma'am is where class comes in. In institutions where there is a strict rank – e.g. the armed services, the court, the police (but not the Civil Service, or universities) – you address those above you as 'Ma'am' (but the salutation in letters is 'Dear Madam' – Ma'am looks stupid on paper). In Britain it's used with a grotesquely open vowel to rhyme with 'salaam' or 'marm(alade)'. In the US, where it's used more promiscuously, the vowel is closed, as in '*Wham, bam, thank you, Ma'am*'.

30. How can a single sentence containing the words 'ate', 'often', 'waistcoat' and 'golf' tell us someone's social class?

Get them to read said sentence aloud. Upper-class pronunciation of these words would result in the following: 'I eight my brekkers, put on me weskit, and, as I offen do, went orff for a round of goff, upper-class twit that I am.' The linguist Alan S. C. Ross published a lively treatise on social-class markers in British speech in 1954, called *How to Pronounce It*. It was picked up and popularised by Nancy Mitford in an article in *Encounter* and, almost overnight, the British became phoneticists. The ear, despite the decline of received pronunciation, is still the best diagnostic tool for identifying social class in the UK – less so in the US, where accent tends to be regional.

31. 'Waitress' is a no-no, as is the Scottish 'clerkess'. Does that mean 'princess' should go as well?

One can nimbly vault over this problem with an old linguistic rule of thumb that the tailgate '-ess' should be used on titles, not professions. Lion king (titular) and lioness (working cat) pose a small problem.

Clangers

One could call them 'iron rules' because, when they're dropped, they clang – assuming, that is, you're in the company of people with ears sensitive to grammatical rightness and wrongness. Not all are. The clangers should be avoided not because they always violate sense but because they can, in many situations, lose you respect. There are a radioactive half-dozen. Usual Suspects, all of them.

1. The grocer's / grocers' / grocers apostrophe
2. Confusion between its and it's in writing
3. Confusion, in speech and writing, between lay / lie
4. Misspelling of 'their', 'they're', 'there'

Avoid them as you would a hike through Grimpen Mire. But trample as heavily as you like through post-positional prepositions ('Something,' Winston Churchill supposedly jested, 'up with which I will not put.') And beginning sentences with conjunctions (like this).

I'm not, it's clear, a latter-day Fowlerian but I have some hobbyhorsical prejudices. Saying 'between you and I', for example, gives me the creeps, as does pronouncing the letter 'H' as 'haitch', rather than 'aitch'. More interesting, perhaps (one thinks of Woody Allen, in *Bananas*, declaring Swedish to be the new national language), are reforms I'd dearly like to bring in.

1. Forecast punctuation as in Spanish, e.g. *¿Por qué?* And *¡Qué susto!* It's self-evident why.
2. A resurrection of 'thou / thee / thine', to do, as they once did (for Shakespeare), what *'tutoyer'* still does in French and the informal *'du'* does in German. One does not address a five-year-old in the same way one addresses one's boss. One could make do without the Spanish honorary (*'usted(es)'*) form of address.
3. Pace-markers, to convey, in writing, the speed and pace of utterance. How this could be done without mutilating typography, I don't know.
4. A marker for 'irony' (saying one thing, meaning another) so you could notate 'You clever bastard' when it's ironic or unironic.
5. A Zulu click for hyphens. As in 'spear [click] holder'.
6. I'm in two minds about German capitalising of all nouns, not just proper nouns. I like the sense of order (*Reihenfolge* – getting in line) it imposes. Goethe's dying words *'mehr Licht, mehr Licht'*

seem more worthy of the occasion than 'more light, more light', which might well be understood as asking someone to kindly turn on the (death)bedside lights.

PUNCTUATIONAL QUESTIONNAIRE

On with the quiz:

32   On the cover of David Marsh's delightful book, *For Who the Bell Tolls*, the difference between **'Let's eat, grandma!'** and **'Let's eat grandma!'** is noted as a key punctuational dilemma in the search for grammatical perfection. Is that right?

33   Despite his publisher's use of them on his cover, Marsh has little time for **the exclamation mark** (!): they are, he says, **'seldom, if ever, obligatory'**. The biopic film of Keats's life is called *Bright Star*. The Keats poem from which the title is taken opens 'Bright Star!'. Was Keats wasting ink?

34   What's an **em-dash**? What other dashes are there in normal use?

35 **Lower case**? **Upper case**? What are they?

36 'Neither London nor New York will be Livable in Ten Years' Time.' (*Spectator* headline, 25 April 2015). 'A blind patient in Minnesota has been given an implant which has allowed him to see his wife for the first time in ten years.' (*ITN-online*, 15 February 2015). Why *years* in one case and *years'* in the other?

37 What's an **Oxford comma**?

38 *Finnegans Wake* — the most famous missing apostrophe in literature. Is James Joyce's error defensible?

39 '**Perverted commas**', James Joyce wittily called them. Is there any difference between **"double"** and '**single**' usage?

40 While we're on the subject (skip this question if you're getting dots before the eyes), what's the rule about '**full stops and commas *outside* the terminal quote marks**'. OR '**full stops and commas *inside* the terminal quote marks.**'?

41 George Orwell wrote a whole novel; defiantly eschewing the **semi-colon**. What, if anything, was lost?

42 What is **'up-talking'** (also known as HRT, 'high-rise terminal') and what interesting punctuational dilemma does it pose?

43 What's the first grammatical error in the King James's Bible?

44 On 18 April 2015, Zoe Williams opened a jaunty piece on the London taxi trade, in the *Guardian*, as follows. How, in print at least, could it be most punctuationally repaired? **'I got an Uber account and now my feelings are more mixed still. Black cab drivers hate them. "Don't make this about us against Uber," said Kevin, 52, a black cabby.'**

45 Steven Pinker's 1995 monograph, *The Language Instinct: The New Science of Language and Mind*, is a book well worth the read (see question 5). What are the grammatical errors in the title? Or are they even errors?

Solutions to questions 32–45

32. 'Let's eat, grandma!' and 'Let's eat grandma!' is a key punctuational dilemma in the search for grammatical perfection. Is that right?

It would be if language existed in a vacuum tube. But this example would be inconceivable in a real world scenario. When spoken aloud, while sitting with grandma at the dinner table, this statement will be addressed only to grandma herself, and she could hardly be expected to serve up granny-burgers for lunch – so the absence of a comma isn't greatly relevant. The un-comma(d) version, one could argue, only makes sense written, and cannibals (Hannibal Lecter may be an exception) don't use email or twitter to invite fellow anthropophagi to their feasts. It's a clinical, not a real-world, example.

33. The exclamation mark is 'seldom, if ever, obligatory'. The Keats poem is titled 'Bright Star!'. Was Keats wasting ink?

Poets love the exclamation mark; Keats frequently used it in his opening lines to give the impression of 'breaking' into verse, as one breaks into song. Journalists on 'quality' papers – like Marsh, style guru of the *Guardian* – despise them because of the association with the 'Gotcha!' school of tabloid headlines.

34. What's an em-dash? What other dashes are there in normal use?

The term originates with printed spacing, 'm' being the longest lower-case letter, used here to represent the longest form of dash. A standard dash is a hyphen (as in 'lower-case'). An en-dash (based on the width of lower-case 'n') indicates a compound formation, as in 'obsessive–compulsive'. An em dash indicates a pause or interruption. The so-called Shandyan dash (named after Laurence Sterne's comic novel) can extend to ten or more m's. (That is an incorrect use of the apostrophe – but how else could it be done?)

35. Lower case? Upper case? What are they?

Manual compositors (typesetters) used to keep their letters in cases. The capital letters were stored in compartments above the small letters, i.e. the 'upper case'. Like five-finger typists using their keyboard they did not have to look to find what they needed.

36. Why *years* in one case and *years'* in the other?

The rule with 'temporal expressions' is simple, logical, but, thank God, falling out of use. The apostrophe is submerged grammar which represents using the words 'years of time'. If you can't rephrase with an 'of' (as you could with the *Spectator*'s grim forecast, 'Ten Years [of] Time', but couldn't with the statement from ITN), our little friend should go hang elsewhere.

37. What's an Oxford comma?

A 'serial comma' – the comma that comes after the penultimate item in a list, where there are three or more listed items; e.g. 'a, b, c, and d'. It's widely ignored, which can lead to occasional ambiguity as in: 'I hate my school teachers, Tom Cruise and Arnold Schwarzenegger' (there are lots of variations on this example). The most thoughtful meditation on the serial comma's rightness or wrongness is in Lynne Truss's *Eats, Shoots & Leaves*. The objection is that the terminal 'and' is a conjunction and cluttering it up with a conjoining comma 'smacks of smug pedantry', as Harry Mount (BA, Oxon) complains. It was first imposed (via what later became *Hart's Rules* – the compositors' commandments) by Oxford University Press typesetters and editors.

38. *Finnegans Wake* – the most famous missing apostrophe in literature. Is James Joyce's error defensible?

Frankly I have no answer. But see the following.

39. Is there any difference between "double" and 'single' inverted comma usage?

The doubles are less prone to visual duplication jarring where adjoining apostrophes are performing different grammatical functions (e.g. Kingsley Amis's punctuational puzzle-piece: 'Those old things over there are my husband's'… or 'husbands'). It can be confusing to have the same punctuation mark for possession (the apostrophe) and expression (the quote mark). Newspapers, where fact, quickly taken on board, matters, tend to use double quote marks. But in novels like *Heart of Darkness*, where the whole book is a quote by Marlow, and every paragraph opens (not closes) with double quote marks, they create a typographic eyesore. Joyce is a fascinating case. In *Ulysses* he used the French-style dash following a paragraph break to indicate quoted speech. As with the offensively missing apostrophe in *Finnegans Wake*, I think it may have been a little Irish rebellion (the big Irish rebellion was going on while he was writing *Ulysses*) against 'King's English'.

40. What's the rule about full stops and commas *inside* or *outside* terminal quote marks?

The Americans have it easy – always inside (and the quotation marks always double, e.g. "…inside.").

In British usage, the punctuation goes inside the speech marks if it forms part of the material being quoted. There is, perplexingly, another school of correct usage which decrees that punctuation goes inside if the sentence contains a main verb, outside if not. A minefield – but 'sense' (what the sentence means) is never at risk which makes the different practices somewhat academic.

41. George Orwell wrote a whole novel; defiantly eschewing the semi-colon. What, if anything, was lost?

It depends who you listen to. If it's Kurt Vonnegut, not much: 'All they do is show you've been to college.' The *Guardian* style book approves of them as a way of creating a bisectional balance between two halves of a sentence (as I've done in the first sentence of the question). But they are rarely used by journalists, writers in too much of a hurry for semi-anythings. Pragmatics use them as 'super commas', or to create a little separation in lists of divergent objects that commas might make too neighbourly with each other. What's fascinating is that poets really love the semi-colon. Wordsworth, for example, plants them everywhere, as end-liners, in his verse. 'Stanza' means 'a room' and the semi-colon is like a half-open, half-closed door. For example in the last, exquisite stanza of Wordsworth's 'Lucy' poems:

> *No motion has she now, no force;*
> *She neither hears nor sees;*
> *Roll'd round in earth's diurnal course,*
> *With rocks, and stones, and trees.*

Was ever the range of punctuational effect used more beautifully, pausing, tentatively, with the semi-colons, a little rush with the comma, to the closure of the full stop. Always a dangerous thing to say; but Orwell is up the spout here.

42. What is 'up-talking' and what interesting punctuational dilemma does it pose?

It's probably Antipodean in origin but was popularised in the 1980s as 'Valley' (i.e. exurban Los Angeles) chick-talk. As the name implies, it is marked by a cute Minnie Mouse-like upward lilt at the end of every sentence. It makes statements sound oddly interrogative, as in the following example from the Urban Dictionary website: 'I'm Irish but because of *Friends*? And *Sex and the City*? I talk like I'm some kind of Valley Girl because of upspeak?'

43. What's the first grammatical error in the King James's Bible?

It's found in the second (and three subsequent) sentences: 'And the earth was without form, and void; and darkness was upon the face of the deep.' Schoolchildren, in my day (when grammar was grammar), used to be instructed not to start sentences with conjunctions, like 'and'. But nowadays the period (full stop) is more often seen as akin to splicing two pieces of rope, rather than severing rope. It's venial – a forgivable offence.

44. How could the following be most punctuationally repaired? 'Black cab drivers hate them. "Don't make this about us against Uber," said Kevin, 52, a black cabby.'

As Lynne Truss, the nation's schoolmistress on such matters, would instruct, cane swishing – 'hyphenate, Zoe, hyphenate!' 'Black-cab driver' would eliminate the implication that apartheid rules on London streets. Luckily, in the e-version of the paper, some sharp-eyed sub put in the necessary hyphenation fix.

45. *The Language Instinct: The New Science of Language and Mind*. What are the grammatical errors in this title?

Colons – as troublesome in grammar as they are in the human body – are not followed by a capital letter. Except sometimes. On the title pages of books, but not in the text that follows (except, sometimes, chapter titles), the capitalisation rule is routinely infringed. It's one of those things that's wrong, but looks right.

Afterthought

There are billions of spoken words for every written word. And punctuation – literally inscribed 'points' – only belongs to the written. In speech, punctuation, of a kind, can be created by stress, pause, pace, timbre, tone and facial expression. The raised hands with two hooked fingers are a semaphore signal for 'Quote!' – but there is nothing equivalent for, say, the comma. 'Eats shoots and leaves' sounds the same as 'eats, shoots, and leaves'. So too (see above) the eating grandma statement(s). Nor, when we speak, is there an oral equivalent to the white space between printed words. None the less, the expressive power of the spoken word (think of our great living actors) has dimensions that print, try as it may, can never quite emulate.

RUDE MECHANICALS, HOORAY HENRIES

*T*he audience laughs watching *Midsummer Night's Dream* – Shakespeare was laughing as well, one suspects – as the rude mechanicals ('cool name for a band,' muses one blogger) mangle the English language. The only way is Warwickshire. Bottom, for example, instructs his fellow horny-handed thespians that they will meet later in the woods, 'and there we may rehearse most obscenely and courageously'.

The joke is the richer because things more obscene than teddy-bears' picnics do indeed happen 'obscurely' in woods – as Bottom, soon to be endowed with an ass's head and the other thing dangling below his jerkin, will find out.

Our use of language bears many identikit markers. Each of us, from childhood on, has an 'idiolect', a style as unique to us as fingerprints or DNA. 'Me' identifiers. Professor Don Foster, a distinguished Shakespearian scholar, helps track the linguistic spoor of the

63

FBI's most wanted by micro-analysing their idiosyncratic speech and writing patterns. The effusions of the Unabomber – fond as he was of rambling messages to the world, before he went on to blast it to bits – were as closely analysed stylistically as any Shakespeare sonnet in Professor Foster's classroom. His work helped nail the murderous bastard. (Caltech, the university on the West Coast where I was then working, was on the bomber's 'to do' list; be on the watch, the security office warned, 'for parcels that ooze'.)

And each of us, to go back to the mechanicals, much as we may try to mask it, has a 'sociolect' – a use of language that 'places' us socially. Where we're coming from, where we belong, where we'd like to belong. It's not a simple thing of upper classes speaking proper and lower classes speaking all wrong. Every grouping has its own 'little language', as Jonathan Swift called them, with its own proprieties and peculiar 'are you one of us?' improprieties.

Boris Johnson, when he meets his former chums from the most preposterously exclusive of Oxford Clubs, the Bullingdon, is reported to roar out (not for our Boris any silent Masonic handshake), 'Bullers! Bullers! Bullers!' 'Lungs like leather, bawls like a bull(er),' as the old Donald McGill cartoon would put it. URP, upper received pronunciation, and 'top-talk' habitually add the '-er' suffix. Boris, over the smashed glass on the Bullingdon table, may well be called 'Jonners'.

> **46** **Boris won himself a Bad Grammar award in 2014 for writing about a fellow airline passenger: 'Myself and a few other passengers felt we needed to keep an eye on the male the whole time, as we were worried about the safety of the crew and other passengers.' Where's the bad grammar?**

Boris's little brother, Jo Johnson, another of the Oxford club, lives near me. I once cheerfully greeted him, on his run (he's fitter than his Boris-Bike brother; impressive calves), with a cheery 'Bullers, JoJo!' He gave me what can only be called 'a look'.

I knew the Johnson look well from army days. In my two years' National Service I rose through the ranks: from 'erk' to 2nd Lieutenant. The little languages of the ranks were proudly different from each other. For the lowly 'other ranks' – the 'chaps' (in officer-speak) – where they 'gonked' (slept), for example, was a 'wanker', sometimes a 'pit' (wankers' pit). Officers, on the other hand, had 'beds' – 'made up' (not just 'made') by their 'batman' (called, in the not so distant past, 'servants').

When tired, officers were 'bushed'. Tired NCOs (with recollections of forced marches in past wars), when exhausted by the day's duties, were 'on their chinstraps' (i.e. helmet chinstraps, holding the jaw clamped, as with a corpse's facial ribbon). The other ranks ('blokes', in NCO-speak) were, pure and simple, 'knackered' – i.e. at the knackers' yard, where horses end their days, on the way to the glue-pot. 'Knackers' is also slang for testicles – there's a secondary gelded implication lurking somewhere.

47   What's the four-letter word, heard everywhere in the army, which can be used, variably, as a noun, a verb, an adjectival modifier and an adverb?

Humphrey Lyttleton recalls that the first lesson he learned as a Guards' officer during 'the' war was never to ask the mess servant for 'a beer', but always 'a glass of beer', which, perversely, would come in a regimental silver tankard. He and his mess-mates would no more ask for 'cha' than hemlock. When a glass too many had been taken in, the officers were 'sloshed', NCOs and ORs, 'pissed'.

Estuary, chav-speak, seems to have risen as an *argot du jour* (cynics noted how Ed Miliband slipped into it

in his epic chat with Russell Brand – two very well-
educated boys talking 'street', glottalising with the
best (?) of them). The Urban Dictionary website gives
the following example of chavery rampant:

*Oi init bruvv, got my 4 by 4 ravers and bass line skankers
init sket. we goin to blow this place out wicked blud. ahhh
mate thats well dog has it bluddd oi lets sketchit yo ay
and hit the legs this is well waffle munter bruv.*

Which it translates (Google Translate having not yet
got round to chav) as 'I'm ready to party. Let's rock
it. This crap let go.' Chav, as with Brand's usage of
it, is more often a spicy flavour of the month than a
coherent dialect in its own right.

Most interesting, most alive and ever changing,
ever obsolescing, is low-life urban speech. 'Gertcha!'
the little street urchin ('street arabs', Victorians
called them) snarled at me just the other day, when
I came between him, his football and the gutter on
Waterloo Road. It had been 60 years since I'd heard
it. 'Seriously?' I thought. It's a locution straight out
of Charles Booth's *Life and Labour of the people in
London* (1889). Eric Partridge, the dictionary maker
who did for slang what Dr Johnson did for 'Standard
English', explains the objurgation in his 1937 glossary:

Gertcher: get out of it, you!

My little unfriend was as likely to say 'avaunt!', as did his Elizabethan predecessors, as 'get out of it, you!' 'Gertcha' was quaint. Where did he pick it up? A wizened grandfather, muttering toothlessly, by the hearth? You still hear 'wotcha, mate' (descendant of 'what cheer, my friend?') among what the Americans call RGWs, 'regular working guys'. In America itself the descendant of 'what cheer?' (which the Puritans must have brought with them on their glum voyage west) is 'howyadoin?'. To which the answer is, with an upward toss of the head, a reciprocally cheerful 'I'm good'. St Peter may think differently.

Dickens had a finely tuned ear for street talk (he had been a street arab himself once) and stretched the sadly limited elasticity of print to capture its orthographic wrongdoings. The Artful Dodger's opening words to well-spoken Oliver (proper English is in the little fellow's DNA) swirl up from the page like the sharp aroma from a whelk-stall:

'Hullo, my covey! What's the row?' said this strange young gentleman to Oliver.

'I am very hungry and tired,' replied Oliver: the tears standing in his eyes as he spoke. 'I have walked a long way. I have been walking these seven days.'

*'Walking for sivin days!' said the young gentleman.
'Oh, I see. Beak's order, eh? But,' he added, noticing
Oliver's look of surprise, 'I suppose you don't know what
a beak is, my flash com-pan-i-on.'*

*Oliver mildly replied, that he had always heard a
bird's mouth described by the term in question.*

'My eyes, how green!' exclaimed the young gentleman.

---

48   What's a deictic?

Fowler has a nice term for street talk – which, in
his view, is where it should stay. He calls it 'slang',
language never to be used in good company. But the
great arbiter pays the unclean thing an odd compli-
ment. 'The place of slang is in real life', he says.

Top-people in England – insulated by heredi-
tary wealth, class inbreeding and unearned prestige
– speak dialect as old and stately as their country
houses. There is no need ever to remove the plum
from the mouth. Privilege has bubble-wrapped them
from any contact with Fowler's real world. As for
living (language), to paraphrase Marie Antoinette,
their servants talk it for them. Where is the 'real-life'
vitality of language – upstairs, in the drawing room of
Downton Abbey, or downstairs?

49   'Did you want something, My Lady?' says the obsequious butler, Carson, having been 'rung' upstairs. Why not 'Do you want something, My Lady?'

When Prince Harry was born, a town crier dressed in full eighteenth-century fig stood on the steps of St Mary's hospital to announce, bellowingly, 'O Yea! O Yea! Their Royal Highnesses wish to announce that unto the nation a spare is born', or words to that effect. 'Who is this guy always yelling at Royal Births?' asked the *Huffington Post*, in republican bewilderment.

How, then, as E. M. Forster would say, to 'connect' in an age when linguistic barriers are falling (the BBC has newscasters nowadays whose street and regional tones would shrivel Alvar Lidell's tonsils)?

There are ways not to do it. The mind shudders at the thought of Prince Charles taking 'fix it' advice on his forthcoming speeches from Jimmy Savile – for whom HRH was 'his nibs', and Diana 'my number one girl'. ('Nibs', by the way, has altered – by generational 'i mutation' – from 'nobs'. Short for 'nobility', vulgar-ised, via another linguistic route, into the Gallagher brothers' favourite term of insult, 'knob'. 'Number one girl' alludes, of course, to Savile's hosting role in TOTPs, Top of the Pops, and the totties he liked to surround himself with. The beast.)

In reality, the only change in royal-speak that speech archivists have noted is a slight relaxation of the top-speak 'sliding vowel' in Prince William's usage – nothing significant and self-explanory (sic).

Solutions to questions 46–49

46. 'Myself and a few other passengers felt we needed to keep an eye on the male the whole time...' Where's the bad grammar?

I can't do better than cite N. M. Gwynne (author of *Gwynne's Grammar*, 2012): '"Myself" absolutely cannot be used other than as an intensive pronoun or any reflexive pronoun... And "male" is used expressly to distinguish a member of the male sex from a member of the female sex; not just to indicate any old person of the male sex.' BoJo is reputed to earn £250k a year from the *Telegraph*. Mr Gwynne published a crusty grammar test, in 2013, in the same newspaper. One suspects they paid rather less.

47. What's the four-letter word?

It's the archetypal four-letter word, as in: 'He's an absolute fuck' (noun) / 'She'll fuck anyone' (verb)

/ 'What a fuck-awful concert that was' ('fuck' modifies the adjective 'awful') / 'He drives like fuck' (adverbial phrase). The film *Four Weddings and a Funeral* opens with Hugh Grant's exclamative 'Fuck! Fuck! Fuck!' where it's as ungrammatical as a belch. A very hard-working word. It was emancipated for authors to use, without fear of prosecution, in the *Lady Chatterley* trial of November 1960.

48. What's a deictic?

Dickens loved them. The simplest definition is a word which 'points'. Take the opening of Dickens's *Bleak House*: 'London.' It's not a sentence (no subject-verb-object), not an adjective. One can riffle through all the parts of speech without finding a good definition. It simply points towards London.

49. 'Did you want something, My Lady?' says Carson. Why not 'Do you want something, My Lady?'

It's polite, infers a degree of subservience, but it also embodies what one might call 'narrative grammar'. My Lady chose, a few minutes ago (or longer), to pull the bell cord, with the aim of something being done for her (a grape peeled, or whatever). Her faithful retainer's 'did' gracefully acknowledges that little back-story

Thug Grammar

*L*anguage, frozen by tradition and heritage at the top, boils ceaselessly at the bottom. A street language which has gripped me over the last 20 years (much of it spent listening to FM radio, on California freeways – lovely word) is Rap. The word itself is linked to 'rapport', making contact, and gunshot (rat-a-tat-tat).

The artists (poets, the best of them) call it 'slanging' and 'rhyming'. The lyrics are strictly word-based, not instrumental, apart from background percussion and disc scraping.

Rap has, to my ear, brutal vitality; it's life force five on the verbal hurricane scale. One of the most beautiful of 2Pac Shakur's lyrics, *Changes* (he composed all his own words – often spontaneously) climaxes on the melancholy injunction:

We gotta make a change…

It's time for us as a people to start makin' some changes.
Let's change the way we eat, let's change the way we live
and let's change the way we treat each other.
You see the old way wasn't working so it's on us to do
what we gotta do, to survive.

This was recorded ('dropping the jewel', as 2Pac calls it) and remixed in the nineties. In the same historical period, the 42nd president, William Jefferson Clinton, was 'dropping', more leadenly, his 1996 state of the union address to Congress. 'I challenge all our schools,' he intoned:

to teach character education, to teach good values and
good citizenship. And if it means that teenagers will stop
killing each other over designer jackets, then our public
schools should be able to require their students to wear
school uniforms.

The same message, 'gotta, gotta, gotta', from the Capitol to South Central, Los Angeles. But in two languages separated by a gulf so wide that, as 2Pac glumly says, 'things ain't never gonna change'.

KINGLY (QUEENLY) ENGLISH

'*W*e have become a grandmother!' Mrs Thatcher's proud announcement to the world, in 1989, on the birth of her first grandchild. Arrogant, indubitably, forgivable, certainly – but ungrammatical? Grandma has, in the excitement of the moment, invoked the royal 'we' (used in public address). As phrases.org.uk wittily observes, 'Its use by a mere prime minister and Thatcher's imperious personal manner were the source of considerable disdain at the time.' Thatcher's apparent conceit led to her being described as 'a legend in her own imagination' and to some linguistic jokes at her expense, e.g. 'Why is Margaret Thatcher like a pound coin? – Because she is thick, brassy and thinks she's a sovereign.' Popes have traditionally used the papal 'we', less so recently after John Paul I went egoistic. Pope Francis caused a bit of a stir when he reverted to it. Obama was accused in his 2009 inauguration speech of *pluralis majestatis*, when he said, 'We will build the roads and bridges.' But he did not, of course, say 'we are a bridge-builder'.

Our language is called the Queen's English in deference to its notional owner. But when, to risk *lèse majesté*, did QE2 ever say anything interesting, or quotable, outside an Alan Bennett play? Shakespeare, for whom the killing and replacement of kings (and, in one case, a queen – Cleopatra) mattered, made his royals fluent in ways that their real-world equivalents have never been. Royal talk is one of the many rich veins in the plays.

From whatever direction one approaches it, *King Lear* is the most profound of Shakespeare's tragedies. Lear (kinged and unkinged) has a telling career in grammar during the course of the action. In the first scene, before his abdication, his grammatical tone is royally imperative:

Come not between the dragon and his wrath!

he thunders, after Cordelia declines to pay the filial tribute his majesty expects. In the height of his madness, on the heath, Lear commands even the heavens, as if he were Zeus himself, with meteorological thunder at his bidding:

> *Blow, winds, and crack your cheeks! rage! blow!*
> *You cataracts and hurricanoes, spout*
> *Till you have drench'd our steeples, drown'd the cocks!*
>   *[i.e. weathercocks]*

At the end the man who was once 'King Lear', is 'a poor, bare forked animal'. And he humbly invites, not commands, Cordelia to join him in captivity:

> *No, no, no, no! Come, let's away to prison.*
> *We two alone will sing like birds i' th' cage.*
> *When thou dost ask me blessing, I'll kneel down*
> *And ask of thee forgiveness.*

Imperative has become implorative: 'Let's away.' 'You' has become the humbly intimate 'thee'. Verb and pronoun say more than any eloquence, even Shakespeare's, could. Rhetoric uncrowned.

Some everyday phrases put through the grammatical wringer

Professor Bas Aarts parses some of our most common sayings to show how everyday sentences are structured, and how, even in the most casual use of language, grammar is always at work…

1. 'Get lost'

There is a whiff of the passive voice to this sentence, which is why it is sometimes called a 'pseudo-passive'. When we want someone to do something for us we can use an imperative in English, as in 'eat your dinner', 'close the door', 'don't pick your nose'. As you can see, imperatives do not have a subject, though in most cases 'you' is implied as being the addressee. 'Get lost' is also an imperative, and quite a rude one at that. From the point of view of grammar it's a bit unusual because it involves the adjective 'lost', which expresses a state, after the verb 'get'. 'Get lost' means 'get yourself in a state of being lost'.

2. 'It's all over now'

This sentence contains the pronoun 'all' which is called a 'floating quantifier'. What's that? The floating quantifier is a curious phenomenon in English in that it is placed after a verb, even though it really belongs with (before) the subject of the sentence – in this case 'it'. We interpret the sentence to mean 'All (of) it is over now'. We also see 'all' as a floating quantifier in a sentence like this: 'The students all hated the performance.' Here the quantifier has drifted away from the subject 'students', and should read: 'All the students hated the performance.' What about 'over' and 'now'? The former is an adjective, the latter an adverb.

3. 'My heart bleeds for you'

From a grammatical point of view this is quite a straightforward sentence: first we have a metonymic subject 'my heart' (where a part represents the whole), followed by a meta-phorical intransitive verb 'bleed'. Intransitive verbs are verbs that do not have a direct object following them. Other such verbs are 'blush', 'smirk', 'swoon'. (Transitive verbs, conversely, require an object, as in 'have', 'give', 'take'.) The prepositional phrase 'for you' functions as an adverbial. See? Easy...

4. 'What goes around comes around'

Relative clauses in English give us more information about the nouns that they relate to. So, in the sentence 'I saw the politician w*ho was jailed for fraud*', the italicised portion is a relative clause which relates to the noun 'politician', using the relative pronoun 'who'. In '*what goes around* comes around', the italicised part, which contains a relative clause, is grammatically tricky. We interpret 'what goes around' as '*that* which goes around'. What has happened here is that the noun 'that' and its relative clause 'which goes around' are fused into one giving us 'what goes around' (with the word 'that' now rendered invisible). The latter part of the saying ('*comes around*') is called a 'free relative clause'. Why 'free'? Because there is no overt word to which the relative clause relates, and that's because the word 'that' has been absorbed into the first half of the sentence.

5. **'High fences make good neighbours'**

Here the subject of the sentence is 'high fences', which is followed by the verb 'make' and what looks like a direct object, namely 'good neighbours'. But this is not really the right way to look at this sentence, because obviously high fences can't 'make' anything, in the way that a human being can make something (as in 'I made a phone call', 'we will make an agreement', etc). So what is going on here? What we have is a special use of the verb 'make' that we also find in, for example, 'she makes a great president'. It seems to combine two meanings, namely 'constitute' and 'be'.

6. 'I know I'm not supposed to'

This is an elliptical sentence, said in response to someone saying, for example, 'Why on earth did you play tennis naked?' The full response would then be, 'I know that I'm not supposed to play tennis naked (but I couldn't help myself).' How do we analyse the full sentence? Here the subject is 'I' which is followed by the verb 'know'. This verb in turn is followed by a clause, namely 'that I'm not supposed to (play tennis naked)', which functions as its direct object.

7. 'Something happened'

This sentence has the indefinite pronoun 'something' as its subject, representing an as yet undefined, and probably unexpected, event. It is followed by the intransitive verb 'happen', which as we have seen, is complete without an object.

8. 'He's gone without trace'

The combination of an apostrophe and 's' (–'s) has two main uses in English. One of these indicates possession, as in 'Harry's shirt', or 'Naomi's trainers'. The other signals the verb 'be' contracted onto the word before it, as in 'he's nice', 'she's playing tennis'. (Of course, 'am' ends up as 'm, as in 'I'm', and 'you are', 'we are' and 'they are' become 'you're', 'we're' and 'they're'.) In this example we have 'he is gone', where 'gone' is an adjective in the form of a past participle which expresses a state. What about 'without trace'? We call this a prepositional phrase, formed in this instance by the preposition 'without' and the noun 'trace'.

9. 'I feel bad about this'

In English there are a number of verbs that can be followed by an adjective. Among them are 'be', 'seem', 'appear' and 'feel'. Of these, the verb 'feel' expresses a sensation or perception. This kind of verb does not take a direct object. What about the adjective 'bad'? Isn't that a direct object? No, it isn't, because direct objects usually refer to people or things that are being 'acted upon'. So, in 'I drank my coffee', the coffee was being drunk, and as a result we say that this phrase functions as a direct object. By contrast, in 'I feel bad about this' the adjective 'bad' functions as a subject complement. Such complements tell you more about the subject of the sentence, in this case 'I'.

10. 'That's all, folks'

Here we have the apostrophe and 's' again, which act as a shorthand for the verb 'is', clipped onto the subject 'that'. The pronoun 'all' is again the quantifier that we came across in 'it's all over now', but this time it's the non-floating kind. The noun 'folks' is called a vocative, which we use to address people. These are usually proper names, as in 'Greg, are you here?', but nouns are very common as well.

Ain't Ain't Always the Baddest Grammar

*O*ne of the acid-test social-status markers in the past was the verb 'ain't'. It won't offend one's ears nowadays as much as it used to. It has been largely bleached out from well-meaning common usage by education and upward mobility. The process has been aided by nationally broadcast language in radio, TV and film.

'Ain't' is a vulgar condensation of, 'are not', 'is not', and sometimes 'has not' (the analogous usage 'han't' has been centuries' out of use). The fact that it is so elastic partly explains its survival.

As Wikipedia (which has an excellent entry on 'ain't') tells us, it's been labelled 'the most stigmatized word in the language'. It 'places' its user. Often ethnically. Usually degradingly. But the word itself, in certain contexts, can fly above everyday speech into its own kind of poetry.

Consider the following famous examples (there will be a jingle in your ears and a tap in your feet, as you read them):

'It ain't necessarily so'
    – Ira Gershwin

Ain't she sweet
Just a walkin' down the street?
Now I asks you kinda confidentially
Ain't she sweet?
    – Jack Yellen

It ain't no sin,
To take off your skin
And dance around
In your bones.
    – Tom Waits

It don't mean a thing if it ain't got that swing
    – Duke Ellington

'You ain't heard nothin' yet'
    – Al Jolson (in black face, in Hollywood's first 'talkie' sequence, having sentimentally crooned 'Mammie!')

Is you is, or is you ain't, my baby?
— Louis Jordan

Ain't no sunshine when she's gone
— Bill Withers

What would be lost if the above song snippets were de-stigmatised into: 'Are you, or are you not, my sweetheart?', 'There's no sunshine when she's gone', etc? Choose your word for the loss: 'linguistic fibre', 'texture' — best of all, probably, 'livingness'. One avoids the radioactive term 'colour'. It evokes, uncomfortably, Al Jolson's 'blackface' (always printed as one word — he didn't have a 'black face').

> 50   One of the red-line rules still taught schoolchildren is to avoid double negatives. Is there any defence for two of the most famously chanted of our time: 'We don't need no educashun' and 'I caint get no sadisfacshun'?

Elsewhere colourful is good. Language can, with too much 'correctness', purify into something as lifelessly blank as Esperanto, as tasteless as distilled water. The above uses of the word 'ain't' are charged with something more than their total of 32 letters and eight punctuational symbols can typographically convey.

President Obama, oddly, is very fond of 'ain't', and uses it with sly POTUS (President of the United States) authority, as when, in the build-up to the Independence Vote, he told the Scottish people, 'If it ain't broke, don't fix it.'

After the leader of Al Qaeda had been 'fixed', someone spoofing Obama tweeted, 'I got 99 problems but Osama ain't one.' As everyone under the age of 30 apprehended, the reference was to Jay Z's raunch-rap hit which opens:

If you're having girl problems I feel bad for you, son
I got 99 problems but a bitch ain't one

The tweet seemed too good not to be genuine, but, of course, it wasn't. Still, for me, the President's form with language, specifically the word 'ain't', made it seem somehow plausible.

There's a veritable banquet of aintery in North Korea's least favourite film, *The Interview*. It's the story of two sub-MTV talk-show guys (their recent hit interviews have been 'Eminem is gay' and 'Matthew McConaughey fucks goats') who are charged by the CIA to assassinate Kim Jong Un – a secret fan of their show.

The show's producer, Aaron Rapaport, wonders why people in their line of the TV business, despite the fact they are watched by millions, including heads of state (didn't Bill play his sax on MTV?), don't have the 'respect' of the people. The presenter Dave Skylark explains, 'They hate us, 'cos they ain't us.' He repeats it defiantly. 'They hate us 'cos they ain't us.' Rapaport demurs. Truth is, he and his colleagues are purveyors of shit for the shit-hungry masses: 'They hate us because we is us and what we're doing is fucking terrible.'

Ain't, one can say, ain't over yet.

Solution to question 50

50. Is there any defence for the double negatives in 'We don't need no educashun' and 'I caint get no sadisfacshun'?

They are not, *in situ*, double negatives in the logical sense 'neg+neg = positive'; e.g. 'I haven't not thought about this.' They are intensifiers or multipliers of the negativity – something made clear by the choral chanting 'no! no! no!' in the background of the Stones track. Orwell hated the N2, and his mocking example about not unblack dogs chasing not unsmall rabbits across not ungreen fields is tediously cited. More tolerant dictators of style cite Chaucer's and Shakespeare's double (sometimes triple) negatives and Jane Austen's endearing fondness for 'not unseldom'. Simon Heffer, in *Simply English*, notes John Major's penchant for double negatives such as 'not inconsiderable' and how they became more frequent as his not unseldom problems with his colleagues multiplied. Double negatives do not, it should be remembered, obey the rules of logic, so 'I don't know nothing' doesn't mean 'I know something', but notice that 'not inconsiderable' does mean 'considerable', so here two negatives do make a positive.

Jane Austen's grammar

There is a raging debate about Jane Austen. In 2010 Professor Kathryn Sutherland – a distinguished Austen scholar – claimed, from examination of surviving manuscripts, to have 'exploded the myth' of the author's perfect grammar:

> *Austen's unpublished manuscripts unpick her reputation for perfection in various ways: we see blots, crossings out, messiness; we see creation as it happens; and in Austen's case, we discover a powerful counter-grammatical way of writing. She broke most of the rules for writing good English. In particular, the high degree of polished punctuation and epigrammatic style we see in* Emma *and* Persuasion *is simply not there.*

As with many authors, it was editors who polished up the raw material into what is now admired. A corps of Janeites leapt to Austen's defence, but, on the evidence of the manuscripts subsequently reproduced, en masse, by the British Library, Professor K. Sutherland would seem to be in the right and the author of *Pride and Prejudice* more than occasionally in the wrong.

TEST TWO

51   Saucy Kingsley Amis offers two sentences, one of which is correct, the other incorrect. (1) **'Samantha is twenty years old and blue-eyed and has a large bust.'** (2) **'Samantha is twenty years old, blue-eyed and has a large bust.'** Which is correct?

52   What is **periphrasis**?

53   **'John went to the cricket match. He himself had no interest in the game'**. 'Himself' doesn't add to the meaning, so what's it doing here?

54   The verb **'adopt'** gives us **'adoption'**; **'adapt'** gives us **'adaptation'**. What's the objection to 'adaption'?

55 **'The Victorians aged faster than us'; 'The Victorians aged faster than we do'.** Obviously 'than us does' is impossible, but why not 'than we'?

56 Spot the grammatical / sense / taste errors crammed into the macabre Post Office brochure, pushing its pre-mortem insurance policies through our letter boxes, with the headline: **'Look After Your Loved Ones When You've Gone!'**

57 **'Tom Brokaw Diagnosed with Bone Cancer: Stars Who Have Battled Cancer'**, ran a sad headline and accompanying pictorial feature in the *New York Daily News*, in August 2013. What grammatical error is there in the headline, if any?

58 What does **'rubric'** mean?

59 Another Bill and Ted question. The duo's message to the universe that their music will one day harmonise (when Wyld Stallyns finally learns a chord or two) is **'Be Excellent to Each Other'**. Is that grammatical, or ungrammatical?

60 **Further versus farther**. The rule distinguishing the near homophones is simple and you certainly know it. How, though, does 'furthermost' complicate the rule?

61 One of Robert Kennedy's most widely quoted utterances is: **'Each time a man stands up for an ideal, or acts to improve the lot of others, or strikes out against injustice, he sends forth a tiny ripple of hope, and those ripples build a current which can sweep down the mightiest walls of oppression and resistance.'** A noble sentiment. But should it not be 'Every time...' as in the lovely Ella Fitzgerald song: 'Every time we say goodbye, I die a little / Every time we say goodbye, I wonder why a little'?

62 **'Pete Bush and the hoi polloi'** is the name of an indie / jazz / folk band (check out their website and sampler – I like them). What's the grammatical error?

63 *Who's Who* has, for a century, recorded the country's A-list. But can 'who' grammatically be a noun, as the second 'who' in the title apparently is?

64 **'One never knows, do one?'** Is there any defence of Fats Waller's grammar, other than its cuteness?

65 **'President Obama's Re-election Campaign Is Doing Okay, Money-Wise'** (*New York Magazine*, 2012). What's the grammatical function of the latch-on 'wise' here?

Solutions to questions 51–65

51. 'Samantha is twenty years old and blue-eyed and has a large bust' or 'Samantha is twenty years old, blue-eyed and has a large bust'. Which is correct?

The first, if you go along with Amis (I'm not sure I do, though I'd think twice about disagreeing to his face, laying down grammatical law in the Garrick Club). His reasoning hinges on the use of 'and'. This 'little word', he says, 'is one of the most troublesome in the language and one of the most often misused.' The misuse here arises from the 'false deduction that "and" must only be used once in a sentence and pretty near its end for preference'. In this particular case, the word 'and' connects items in a list, but there are two lists in the sentence, not just the one: the first details two facts (she is twenty and blue-eyed), and the second combines that small list of facts to an observation about her vital statistics (her large bust) – in other words: she is twenty and blue-eyed and she has a large bust. Hence the supposed requirement that there be two 'ands'. And hence what Amis rather unconvincingly calls the 'commonest mistake in written English'.

52. What is periphrasis?

Interesting, and always worth a second look. Close cousin of 'euphemism'. Periphrasis is from the Greek, meaning 'talking around'. In formal grammar it means surrounding a word with other words that add nothing to the meaning (e.g. 'to walk', 'to take a walk', 'go for a walk'). In everyday speech, and literature, the phrasal overload is often suspicious, when it's not highfalutin. It was at its most highfalutin in eighteenth century poetry (e.g. 'finny tribe' for 'fish', 'feathered kind' for bird). Periphrasis can be mealy-mouthed – e.g. 'house of ill repute where ladies of easy virtue are to be found' (brothel, where sexworkers are for sale). Or used to comic effect, such as by comedian Barry Humphries – 'Off to point percy at the porcelain' (Barry McKenzie-speak for 'urinate'). Sometimes the practice indicates sensitivity. For example the move, over the last 30 years, from 'crippled' to 'handicapped' to 'disabled'. Fowler is severe:

> *periphrasis and civilization are by many held to be inseparable. These good people feel that there is an almost indecent nakedness, a reversion to barbarism, in saying 'no news is good news' instead of 'the absence of intelligence is an indication of satisfactory developments'.*

Periphrasis is none the less deeply rooted in the English language: historical linguists trace it, and euphemism, back to the Anglo-Saxon 'kenning'. The most horrible current euphemism – 'Liverpool Care Pathway' – is a hospital term for starving DNR patients to death. DNR? Another euphemism for 'don't bother' – short, in medical acronymese for 'Do Not Resuscitate'.

53. 'He himself had no interest in the game'. 'Himself' doesn't add to the meaning, so what's it doing here?

Two things. First, the reflexive '+self' is an intensifier – hammering the weak pronoun 'he' a bit harder. Second, it serves to create a small space, or semantic blank, for thought (for the speaker and the person spoken to) to catch up with the words spoken. 'I myself [pause]...' is always useful for that purpose.

54. The verb 'adopt' gives us 'adoption'; 'adapt' gives us 'adaptation'. What's the objection to 'adaption'?

'It's coming,' laments Kingsley Amis, adding, 'I mean to continue with adaptation for the moment, but the time will probably come when it will seem first quaint and then unintelligible.' Amis makes a forlorn plea for 'retractation' (not 'retraction'). Two stops beyond quaint, alas.

55. 'The Victorians aged faster than us'; 'The Victorians aged faster than we do'. Why not 'than we'?

As Charles Carson argues on the Quick and Dirty Tips website, there's a centuries'-long battle between 'conjunctivists' who think that 'than' is a conjunction (i.e. joining two statements) and 'prepositionists'. As for the latter Carson explains, 'A preposition is a word that combines with a noun or pronoun to form a phrase that modifies an object or action.' Carson uses the example 'behind him', where you have an object ('him') of a preposition ('behind'). As for the case in question, 'us' is the object of the prepostion 'than' – and thus it must be in the object case ('us' not 'we'). You would say, therefore, 'The Victorians aged faster than us'. If, on the contrary, 'than' is a conjunction, it is joining two statements, 'the Victorians age' and 'we age' (or 'we do'), hence 'The Victorians aged faster than we do'. A little battle for card-carrying grammarians. For others, put in the WTF drawer and move on.

56. Spot the grammatical / sense / taste errors: 'Look After Your Loved Ones When You've Gone!'

This exhortation implies that you would be capable of taking action 'after you're dead and gone', suggesting, in some Amityville horror twist, that you're going to come back and haunt the family home. Technically it can be defended: 'look after' is an imperative, and hence does not have any tense. It's non-finite. But the instruction carries with it a future time implication. For true sense it should be, un-eye-catchingly, 'Ensure that you will have looked after your family, when you're dead, with our insurance scheme'. But, of course, the future perfect tense is a trifle unsexy. As is the word 'dead'. It helps to know where words and phrases come from. Although 'loved one' is now universally used to refer to those for whom you care deeply in life, it originated as a term of sarcasm in Evelyn Waugh's novel about the American way of death, *The Loved One* (1948). Waugh noted the phrase was used as a coy euphemism for 'cadaver' at Forest Lawn, in Los Angeles, the mortuary of the stars. What the Post Office is saying is, 'When you're a corpse, look after your loved corpses'. Forest Lawn's publicity no longer uses the term, I believe.

57. 'Tom Brokaw Diagnosed with Bone Cancer: Stars Who Have Battled Cancer'. What grammatical error is there in the headline, if any?

Simon Heffer argues that there is an error: 'Battle is an intransitive verb. One does not battle cancer, one battles against it, or possibly with it.' At the time of writing, Brokaw is winning his battle. Seems more important than transitivity, somehow.

58. What does 'rubric' mean?

A 'red-line' instruction, at the head or in the margin of a document – initially a medieval manuscript. *The Oxford Dictionary* definition is authoritative: 'Late Middle English *rubrish* (originally referring to a heading, section of text, etc. written in red for distinctiveness)', telling us its sources are Old French (*rubriche*), Latin (*rubrica terra* – 'red earth or ochre as writing material'), and that it comes from the base *rubeus*. You won't improve on that. School-teachers still like to correct in red, book editors (like mine) with the legendary 'blue pencil'.

59. Bill and Ted say, 'Be Excellent to Each Other'. Is that grammatical, or ungrammatical?

Ungrammatical. It should be 'one another'. One couldn't put it more neatly than 'Grammar Girl' does on her Quick and Dirty Tips website. 'The phrase "each other" is known as a reciprocal pronoun because it shows a bidirectional action. For example, if Bill and Ted are being excellent to each other, that means Bill is being excellent to Ted, and Ted is being excellent to Bill. They're practising what you might call excellence reciprocity. But Bill and Ted aren't talking about being excellent just to Bill and Ted; they want each person in the world to be excellent to every other person. According to some grammarians, if we're talking about more than just two people, we should use a different reciprocal pronoun: one another. In other words, Bill and Ted should more properly have said, "Be excellent to one another".' Party on, dudes.

60. Further versus farther. How does 'furthermost' complicate the rule?

A reminder: farther = measurable distance in time and space ('Mars is farther from the Sun than the Earth'); further = distance or separation in an abstract sense ('I have something further to add'). 'Furthermost', however, covers both, because 'farthermost' is a much disliked, and relatively unused, compound. Usage, as ever, trumps rules.

61. 'Each time a man stands up for an ideal [...] he sends forth a tiny ripple of hope.' Should it not be 'Every time'?

'Every' certainly sounds easier on the ear, and obscurely grander, both of which are important in speechifying. But the balance tilts slightly in Kennedy's favour. 'Each' implies singularity – outstandingness – more forcefully. 'Every' carries a larger implication of universality (as for example in 'Everyman Books' – no one's excluded). Kennedy hails the heroic few, not the many. There is only a tiny shade of difference (it wouldn't have been jarring had he said 'each and every time...') but the shade is important.

62. 'Pete Bush and the hoi polloi' – what's the grammatical error?

'*Hoi polloi*' is Greek for 'the people', pejoratised by common usage into 'the plebs' (Latin) and 'low-lifes'. To say 'the hoi polloi' is tantamount to saying 'the the plebs'. If Andrew Mitchell had called the police guarding Downing Street 'effing polloi' he would, quite likely, have saved himself a ton of grief.

63. *Who's Who*. Can 'who' grammatically be a noun, as the second 'who' in the title apparently is?

The Who clearly think it can – but they, in their

heyday, were serial misusers of everything, including, famously, guitars and percussion equipment and, in the case of the drummer, livers. As, for the top-people's directory, Professor Aarts informs me, 'The answer to the question "Can 'who' grammatically be a noun?" is "yes". This word is a pronoun in both cases, and hence a kind of noun.' I take his word for it.

64. 'One never knows, do one?' Is there any defence of Fats Waller's grammar, other than its cuteness?

Cuteness, I fear, has to suffice. 'One' (a tricky pronoun) is singular in reference (e.g. 'one is by oneself on one's desert island'). But while it's often used instead of 'I', it vaguely spreads the assumption in what's being said to others. One could argue, therefore, that the subtext of what Fats is saying, in his disarming childlike falsetto, is 'We never know, do we?' Fats has simply mixed up the usage of the plural and the singular. For cuteness. And ponder, for a moment, why 'Fats' sounds so much friendlier than 'Fatso', or 'Fatty'. I don't have an explanation, but it do, don't it?

65. 'President Obama's Re-election Campaign Is Doing Okay, Money-Wise.' What's the grammatical function of the latch-on 'wise'?

It's an adverbial suffix — it turns a noun into an adverb (a 'like' word). There is a venerable family of them in English usage, e.g. 'likewise', 'clockwise', 'lengthwise'. But noun+wise neologisms began sprouting like weeds in the 1960s and after. As above in the *New York Magazine* article. And everywhere in dude-speak, e.g. 'How's it crumbling, cookie-wise, bro?' My hunch is that it was borrowed, from the more agglomerative German (always a strong influence on American English) where the analogous suffix '*weise*' is very widely used. As in '*geld-weise*' (money-wise).

READ MY LIPS: POL-TALK

*P*oliticians – whose job, as representatives of the people, requires them to speak in many tongues (without apostolic-pentecostal aid from above) – go demotic with the clumsiness, more often than not, of the Johnsonian dog walking on two legs.

When new-dealer Franklin D. Roosevelt told the American people, in one of his radio broadcasts, 'I'm not the smartest fellow in the world, but I can sure pick smart colleagues', it wasn't because Mr President couldn't have come up with something more – let's say – 'presidential'. He wanted to be homely, to get down with the masses crowding round their wirelesses. 'I may well not be the cleverest of men, but I am utterly confident that I can identify the best aides to have around me in my high office' would have missed the mark. It sure would.

Churchill, wisely, kept strictly to the language of his ruling class when speechifying. It worked. The country, in WW2, wanted a leader, not a 'mate' who was 'one of them'.

What in rhetoric is called 'bathos' – sinking, linguistically – has election-losing risks. It is a generally accepted historical fact that Neil Kinnock blew his chances when, at the pseudo-presidential eve-of-election rally at Sheffield, in 1992, he let loose with the repeated bellow 'We're awright!! We're awright!! We're awright!!' A softly spoken 'Aren't things going well for us, comrades? Now let's have a rousing chorus of "The Internationale", to remind us what we stand for' might have been luckier for the Labour Party's 'nearly man' (interestingly ungrammatical phrase, but none fits better). Rant at your peril, wannabe PM.

> 66 'Awright' is unspeakable. But Kingsley Amis has a problem with 'alright'. In *The King's English* he writes (or, as he would say, 'inscribes') fumingly, 'I still feel that to inscribe "alright" is gross, crass, coarse and to be avoided, and I now say so.' Are you with him?

Or wannabe president, as Howard Dean found out when he scuppered his chances of making it by prefacing his speech in West Des Moines, Iowa, during the 2004 Democrat presidential primary campaign, with a Tarzanic yell, rendered onomatopoeically as 'BYAH!' and 'YEARGH!'. It was amplified, ear-splittingly, by a defective sound system. Remorselessly 'mashed' and 'YouTubed', it became immortalised as the 'I have a scream' speech. 'Dean's Scream' is now firmly in the pol-speak glossary, with a skull and crossbones over it.

---

67   **'Yes we can!' was presidential candidate Obama's slogan, in 2008. Forget Republicans. What's the grammarian's objection? And how would the meaning have altered had he said 'Yes we may'?**

It was the cannier Ronald Reagan who, during one of the many Iran crises, universalised the slippery confession: 'I mis-spoke' (i.e. lied my presidential head off). An actor by profession, the 'Great Communicator' misread the script and miscommunicated. No matter. The script doctors would sort it out.

---

68   **George H.W. Bush's campaign slogan in 1992 was 'Who do you trust?' Ungrammatical?**

> **69** **During the 1992 election, Bush versus Clinton, Democrat campaigners handed out lapel badges saying 'Vote Republican. NOT!' What was the allusion, and what is the (un)grammar?**

Donald Rumsfeld, one of Bush II's *consiglieri* gave us that sublime Rumsfeldism:

> *There are known knowns. These are things we know that we know. There are known unknowns. That is to say, there are things that we know we don't know. But there are also unknown unknowns. There are things we don't know we don't know.*

This does to epistemology what tyre-rubber does to hedgehogs. None the less, 'known unknown' has entered the political lexicon and there's a truth (as with Fats Waller's 'one never knows, do one?') lurking in the verbal maze. If he'd said, 'known uncertainties' it would have passed without comment – and never have been immortalised.

Tricky Dick Nixon was a past master of pol-speak, most characteristically when his volcanic paranoia erupted, as when he said (conversationally, off-mike, to a newscaster):

You know, it's a funny thing, every one of the bastards that are out for legalising marijuana are Jewish. What the Christ is the matter with the Jews, Bob? What is the matter with them? I suppose it is because most of them are psychiatrists.

What the Christ indeed. Of the numerous things that are wrong with this rant, the loose application of subject and object leads one to wonder whether Nixon's biggest gripe is with psychiatrists, Jews, or the marijuana legalisers themselves. But the perncickety grammarian in me can't help but note how it should be 'every one... is', not 'are'.

The veritable Houdini of White House pol-speak was the 42nd president (the 'Prez'). It was he, when defending his sex / no sex with the intern, Monica Lewinsky, before the Grand Jury in August 1998, who, in response to a query about his earlier statement 'there is no improper relationship' came up with:

It depends on what the meaning of the word 'is' is. If the— if he— if 'is' means 'is and never has been', that is not— that is one thing. If it means 'there is none', that was a completely true statement.

Wittgenstein would have wrestled with Clinton's

word play. Hamlet could have built a soliloquy round it: 'Is "is" is, or is "is" is not? – that is the question.' But Bill got off. He always did.

> 70   **'I did not have sexual relations with that woman'. What's dangerously loose in Clinton's statement?**

Sometimes, the southerner slipped out past the President's non-inhaling lips, sociolectically, as when he said, unguardedly, in November 1994 (on BET, Black Entertainment TV, of all places), 'African-Americans watch the same news at night that ordinary Americans do.' Generally, though, his control of utterance was master-class. And, at his best, Clinton was genuinely witty, as in an informal moment, he mused about the verbal disciplines high office imposed:

> *Sometimes I feel like the fire hydrant looking at a pack of dogs. For six years I had declined to tell those kinds of jokes, because I have been told it is not presidential. But I feel kind of outdoorsy today.*

The neologism 'outdoorsy' is pitch perfect. And, for a certainty, no scriptwriter put it in his mouth.

Obama speaks, in public, like a professorial robot. One dozes, as, one feels, his back-row Harvard students must have done. At home one can assume his talk is more, to use Michelle's term, 'cheesy' (see above, for his occasional 'aintery'). She was, for the record, referring to his socks.

Obama's doughty opponent in 2008, Sarah Palin, for all her election gaffes, is the most honestly demotic politician of her time. Refreshingly so: a blast of fresh air all the way down from Alaska. Who but Palin would have tweetingly asked (as she did in August 2010):

Who hijacked term: 'feminist'? A cackle of rads who want 2 crucify other women w/whom they disagree on a singular issue; it's ironic (&passé).

'A cackle of rads' ought, surely, to go in the lexicon. And note the 'whom' – I ain't as ungrammatical as I look, buster (demotic for 'you bastard'). And pardon my French, which you didn't know I knew, did you, asshole?

'They' may laugh but Palin refuses to be ashamed of her violations of the English language and the pretzel malapropisms into which she reshapes it. As another salty tweet defiantly asserts:

*'Refudiate,' 'misunderestimate,' 'wee-wee'd up.' English is a
living language. Shakespeare liked to coin new words too.
Got to celebrate it!*

One's reminded of Jacqueline Susann's response,
when questioned about the quality of her prose
(editors are reported to have burst into tears when
her first drafts arrived): 'And when did Shakespeare
ever make #1 on the *New York Times* bestseller list?'
When indeed.

Palin's ritually repeated question to Obama in
office is a magnificent kick in the you-know-where:

*Hey, Mr President How's that hopey, changey stuff working
out for ya?*

The grammarian in me (not, I confess, a dominant
presence in the booth) would vote for Palin, in whose
hands the English language is plasticine.

Of all recent politicians, John Prescott has given
his fellow Britons the richest source of perverse
pol-speak – most of it of the malapropistic, trip-
over-your-own-clogs-and-go-head-first-into-the-
canal kind.

---

71   Who was Mrs Malaprop?

Among the most loved Prescottisms are those that take on a narrative vividness of their own, like his exclamation of his heartfelt relief after a bumpy plane ride: 'It's great to be back on terra cotta.' The prize must, however, go to his dire forecast: 'The sceptre of unemployment is stalking the North East.'

The former deputy PM does to language what Dali does to wristwatches. I miss him, among all the sterile gab of the linguistically constipated PPE graduates at the top of British political life, currently watching their words so carefully that they themselves are not worth watching.

Afterthought

Dismissive as the previous remarks are, one must acknowledge that the most powerful political rhetoric has a quality that is beyond grammatical description. 'Magic' is the only word to use.

Oliver Sacks, the psychologist who boldly goes where no psychologist has gone before, describes a speech given by President Ronald Reagan. Reagan gave many speeches; but this was unusual in that it was given to Sacks's 'Aphasia Ward', to patients who had lost all power of incoming, and outgoing, language. Sacks was alerted by 'a roar of laughter', and went in:

> *There he was, the old Charmer, the Actor, with his practised*
> *rhetoric, his histrionisms, his emotional appeal — and all*
> *the patients were convulsed with laughter... What could*
> *they be thinking? Were they failing to understand him?*
> *Or did they, perhaps, understand him too well?*

The latter, we guess. If it were their friendly doctor, describing their condition, would they respond 'intelligently'? Reagan, the 'Great Communicator', had sublinguistic powers of communication which – dislike Reaganism as we may – 'worked'. The highest kind of praise for language, grammatical or ungrammatical.

Solutions to questions 66–71

66. Amis writes, 'I still feel that to inscribe "alright" is gross, crass, coarse and to be avoided, and I now say so.' Are you with him?

Amis is not alone in insisting on 'all right'. There are many conservative grammarians on his side. I think they are wrong(ish). It may be 'common', but 'alright' avoids the ambiguity which, for example, the title of the (charming) film *The Kids Are All Right* (2010) plays on: i.e. the kids are, every one of them, correct in their opinions about life and their elders; and the kids are OK – alright.

67. 'Yes we can!' What's the grammarian's objection?
Purists insist that a comma is necessary after 'Yes', otherwise it reads like the answer to someone's direct question (e.g. 'can you fix health-care?'). When it comes to using 'can' rather than 'may' we're back in the Grimpen Mire of grammar – the 'can / may' wasteland. Both are permission-granting modal verbs. 'May' is the more polite-sounding. Hence that most irritating kind of conversational one-upmanship – 'Can I go now?' ' You most certainly may.' Lucky French only has the one verb for 'can' and 'may' (*pouvoir*). In English, in their negative forms, 'may' has the stronger permission charge and 'can' the stronger possibility charge. Hence the palpable sense difference between two signposts, one reading 'Visitors May Not Walk on the Grass' (verboten), and the other 'Visitors Cannot Walk on the Grass'. Stephen Hawking, noble man, may, but cannot walk on his college lawn. Go figure, as Americans say.

68. 'Who do you trust?' Ungrammatical?

Yes and no. There were those, of a severe disposi-
tion, who thought it should have been 'Whom do
you trust' – something the Yale-educated candidate knew full well but which Bo Diddly ('Who
do you love?') may, perhaps, not have known.
Or cared about. But politics bends grammar as
routinely as politicians bend truth. Bush wanted
to project a homely Texan old-boy image – there
being more of them among the electorate than
Yalies. 'Read my lips' was George H. Bush's legacy
phrase (recalling, as he surely did not mean to
recall, the joke: 'Q. How do you know a politician's mis-speaking? A. His lips move'). The elder
Bush was clever. 'W', 'Dubbya', following in his
father's footsteps to the Oval Office, was (is) two
thick planks held together by a surname. See the
Bushism: 'Natural gas is hemispheric. I like to call
it hemispheric in nature because it is a product
that we can find in our neighborhoods.'

69. 'Vote Republican. NOT!' What's the allusion, and
what is the (un)grammar?

The allusion is to the slacker talk of Wayne and
Garth in *Wayne's World* (1992), which, for a short
time, became a little rage. (The 'sting-in-the-tail,
post-period' posterior negative – sounds like

115

constipation – in fact had a venerable history.) It soon staled – by the time of the sequel film, *Wayne's World II* (1993), the duo were already sneering at slang laggards who still thought it was smart. 'So 1992' (that use of 'so' is also past its freshest nowadays). For a few months, 'NOT!' rode high and may have garnered Clinton some youth votes. It was selected as the word of the year, in 1992, by the American Dialect Society. You'll find that information very useful. NOT!

70. 'I did not have sexual relations with that woman.' What's dangerously loose in this statement?

The mistake Slippery Willie makes is that he should have said 'I did not have sex with Monica Lewinsky'. He was, however, scared about using her name. The nominally unfixed 'that woman' allows for the interpretation (which POTUS certainly did not intend): 'I did not have sexual relations with that particular dog Monica, or whatever her name is, but I sure as hell diddled a few other better-looking White House aides (heh, heh!).' He should have kept his language better zipped.

71. Who was Mrs Malaprop?

The epically mis-speaking character in Sheridan's comedy, *The Rivals*. Two of the lady's most malapropos malapropisms are 'He is the very pine-apple of politeness' and 'I have since laid Sir Anthony's preposition before her'.

GOVE(RNMENT) GRAMMAR

❖═◎═❖

*G*ood Grammar became, in the Tory years from 2010 onwards, a political cause. It was the equivalent of Mrs Thatcher's 'Victorian Values' as the sour-tasting, 'good for you' medicine Britain sorely needed to put the greatness back in the nation's trousers.

Michael Gove, as Secretary of State for Education, spearheaded his party's drive to bring back correctness into the classroom and, by dissemination over future years, into British society as a whole. Grammar would do for Britain, increasingly fragmented by immigrant tongues, what mortar does for bricks. Unify. Good Grammar, 'GG', would make 'we're all in this together' something more than a slogan.

The principal Tory-supporting national newspaper, the *Daily Telegraph*, lent its considerable moral weight to the Gove GeeGee-up! campaign with a 'Good Grammar Test'. Now was the time for all (grammatically) good men (and, of course, their lady wives) to come to the aid of the party. Check the first three questions out:

Which of these sentences is grammatically correct?
    Do you see who I see?
    Do you see whom I see?

'That was a near miss.' What part of speech is 'near'?
    Noun / Adjective / Verb / Adverb

Which of these sentences is grammatically correct?
    He had less men than in the previous campaign.
    He had fewer men than in the previous campaign.

Mr Gove's crusade for grammatical goodness provoked the ire of the People's Laureate for Children's Literature, Michael Rosen, who took to the comment-is-free columns of the *Guardian* to launch a tooth-and-nail counter-attack against Goveian grammatical authoritarianism. It went ding-dong, as Gove fired back letters to the paper (did not the *Guardian* itself have a 'style sheet'? he slyly enquired).

Rosen concluded:

I think there is one certain way to make life harder for children to acquire Standard English: creating tests that fail hundreds of thousands of children. This is Michael Gove's contribution to 10- and 11-year-olds' linguistic skills.

On Rosen's far left flank, John Harris, a *Guardian* political columnist, galloped into the fray, endorsing 'Wanker's Grammar' as something healthily anti-authoritarian. In 2014 the post-punk Nottingham band Sleaford Mods published some of their lyrics in a limited edition collection called *Grammar Wanker*. It was something of a WG manual, including such politicised ditties as 'Austerity Dogs', 'Urine Mate: Welcome to the Club' and 'Fizzy'. These are the 'lyrics' (not quite the right word) of the last:

The **** with the gut and the Buzz Lightyear haircut calling all the workers plebs, you better think about your future, you better think about your neck, you better think about the shit hairdo you got mate, I work my dreams off for two bits of ravioli and a warm bottle of Smirnoff under a manager that doesn't have a clue, do you want me to tell you what I think about you ****? I don't think that's a very good idea do you?

The grammatical wanker-in-chief is, of course, Russell Brand, with his ten million 'followers' (on Twitter) and his barrage of 'Trews' (a version of the antique slang expletive 'strewth' and the more antique 'God's Truth!'). Looking at and listening to the Sleaford Mods items and Brand-speak, I find myself drifting Govewards. Trewly I do.

The battle had died down by the time the 2015 election reached crunch point. No party included a grammar item in their manifesto.

GRAMMARLESSNESS

*W*anker's versus Gove(rnment) Good Grammar emerges, if one stands back, as a battle of the generations. On another front the young are leading language into areas where the writ of grammar is virtually irrelevant. At some point in the future, I predict, you'll be able to put into the Google Translate programme:

2b????????????

and out will come (with audiovisual accompaniment) Laurence Olivier's fruitily baritone delivery of the most famous line in English Literature:

To be or not to be, that is the question

One of the fun, but sometimes terrifying, things for observers of language in the present age is how unprecedentedly fast it's evolving. Biology was revolutionised when scientists discovered the fruit fly, whose life-cycle, embryo to corpse, lasts only hours, and whose species can take only months to make the evolutionary jumps that take Homo sapiens millennia.

> 72   'Unfriend' is a word (and act) invented and universalised by Facebook and its two billion users. What, the strict grammarian might argue, should be the word?

> 73   While we're down with the kids: 'Duh!' Where did it originate, what does it mean and what does it do? How is it distinguished from 'D'oh!'?

The English language is, at the moment, in its own state of fruit-fly change and adaptation to fast developing new technologies. The hottest of hot houses in which this evolutionary change can be seen happening, almost by the week, is mobile phone text ('txt'). It began as space-compressed language. One hundred and forty 'characters' were all the early generation phones allowed. A matter of bytes. Txt splintered and, where it could, abolished all the finer points of language. Poetry, said Walter Pater, tends towards the condition of music. All txt tends towards the condition of emoticon.

'Less' is the guiding principle of txt – together with 'more', as in the speed of keyboard punch and the to and fro of messages. Txt has, in the process, created a system in which grammatical complexity is reduced to zero, or less. Language point null. The young, as they do in sport, have a speed advantage, and the younger the dog, the more adept it is at picking up new tricks. Old dogs? DBA (don't bother asking).

Solutions to questions 72–73

72. 'Unfriend.' What, the strict grammarian might argue, should be the word?

You can't 'friend' someone. It should be 'unbe-friend'. Some hopes. Four billion ears aren't listening.

73. 'Duh!' Where did it originate, what does it mean and what does it do? How is it distinguished from 'D'oh!'?

These are pure performatives, as J. L. Austin

calls the category of language. Call them 'belch words', expletives. What 'duh!' does, voiced *basso profundo*, is intimate, sarcastically, 'you prat, you'; less often 'oops, what a prat am I'. 'D'oh', having been around for some time, took off in the 1960s. It's now associated with one speaker, Homer Simpson. The Wikipedia entry, clearly written by a Simpsonophile, notes that the word was received into the *Oxford English Dictionary* in 2001, where it is defined as an 'informal exclamation... used to comment on an action perceived as foolish or stupid'. In the show's scripts it is entered as 'annoyed grunt'. Pretty much Homer's response to the mysteries of life.

The txting lexicon

How many of the following acronyms (non-grammatical lexical items) could you, without the answers attached, 'spell out' into 'proper' grammatical English.

1. BRB (Be right back)
2. G2G (Got to go)
3. GR8 (Great)
4. TTYL (Talk to you later)
5. L8RZ (See you later)
6. BBZ (Babe)
7. M8 (Mate)
8. WUUT (What are you up to?)
9. NB (Not bad)
10. NW (No worries)
11. TMB (Text me back)
12. 2NYT (Tonight)
13. Enuf (Enough)
14. ROFL (Rolling on the floor laughing)
15. Sup? (What's up?)

The living acronym

As I write, the top ten 'trending' TACs (text acronyms) are:

1. ORZ
2. INTP
3. DIP
4. BOOMM
5. TGFG
6. PREE
7. TEVS
8. HWB
9. JUAD
10. ONNA

Look them up if you don't know. But by the time you find what they mean they'll be untrended; or consigned to the text trash-can along with Tommy Handley's ITMA. The TAC hovers on the borderline where linguistic meets semiotic – sign language. But it lives, to borrow the title of the classic horror movie. My God, it lives. Most probably in your child's bedroom.

POETRY: THE GRAVEYARD
OF GRAMMAR

O ne of Robert Browning's poems, 'A Grammarian's Funeral', laments the sterility of a life spent
studying grammar, to the exclusion of living to the full:

> So, with the throttling hands of death at strife,
> Ground he at grammar;
> Still, thro' the rattle, parts of speech were rife:
> While he could stammer
> He settled Hoti's business let it be!
> Properly based Oun
> Gave us the doctrine of the enclitic De,
> Dead from the waist down.

Poets exult, each and everyone of them, in killing
the eunuch Grammarian, rejoicing at his funeral,
and dancing on his / her grave. Browning himself,
as above, is flagrantly ungrammatical ('Ground he at

grammar'?). But my uncontroversial nomination for the most wilfully, and beautifully, ungrammatical lyric poem in English is e e cummings's (the man couldn't even be grammatical about his own name) 'anyone lived in a pretty how town':

> *anyone lived in a pretty how town*
> *(with up so floating many bells down)*
> *spring summer autumn winter*
> *he sang his didn't he danced his did.*

Sic, sic, sic and yet more *sic*. Autocheck screams in agony against prepositional madness. Less *lapsus grammaticae* than *collapsus grammaticae*. But it's because he knows the grammatical crimes he's committing that cummings can get away with it. And because, of course, he is testing the limits of 'received' language. Creating literary art as he goes. 'Refreshing the language of the tribe', as the French poet Mallarmé put it: the poet's mission.

---

74   **One for the Dylanologists. Is their man's 'Lay, Lady, Lay' an offence to grammar?**

Verse is constantly engaged in a tug of war with, on one side, the limits of language, teetering on the verge of 'nonsense poetry' (which, frankly, 'anyone lived' is), and, on the other side a tug to the grammarlessness of imagism. Ezra Pound, for example, whittled down a long poem, 'In a Station of the Metro' into the exquisite, verbless pictogram:

The apparition of these faces in the crowd;
Petals on a wet, black bough.

The grammatical nakedness touches the sensibility into a kind of quiet visual explosion.

---

75 What's a 'kenning'?

The *Encyclopaedia Britannica* would be too short for this topic but I'll finish with one more example, from the British nation's favourite poet, Philip Larkin, and his painfully autobiographical poem, 'Dockery and Son'. He's just, in middle age, visited his Oxford college – a mournful experience, seeing the ghost of his youthful self, so hopeful then. And now? Don't ask. Well, if you must:

Life is first boredom, then fear.
Whether or not we use it, it goes,
And leaves what something hidden from us chose,

And age, and then the only end of age.

That comma between 'it' and 'it' would get a nod of teacherly approval from Lynne Truss. But, despite the splice mark, the repetition of 'it' is stutteringly ugly. Why not, 'Whether or not we use it, life goes'? There would be no loss of meaning and a gain in euphony. But Larkin wanted 'dreary' repetition: same thing, day in, day out. In short, it's bad grammar, it's good poetry. And a hefty kick at the grammarian's coffin.

Solutions to questions 74–75

74. Is Dylan's 'Lay, Lady, Lay' an offence to grammar? You lie down on the bed, you lay something on its flat surface (e.g. an eiderdown). The college-educated Dylan knows that, but he wants to suck some juice out of the demotic meaning of 'lay' – as in Dorothy Parker's sardonic 'If all the girls at Vassar were laid end to end I should not be surprised'. 'Lay' also has the secondary meaning 'song'. Songster's licence.

75. What's a 'kenning'?
An Old Norse and Old English poetic device,

where two words are combined to describe something figuratively. The British Library learning site offers the following Anglo-Saxon examples: bone-house (*bānhūs*) – the human body; battle-light (*beadolēoma*) – sword; wave-floater (*wægflota*) – ship. A third of the text of the poem *Beowulf* is made up of kennings. New kennings are being invented all the time: e.g. 'First Lady' (Eve?), 'gas-guzzler' (suicide victim?), 'bullshit merchant' (fertilizer wholesaler?).

LINGUISTIC LEGO

*T*he English language is truly bolted together, with meaning often dictated not so much by the root of the word, as by the little stuck-on pieces placed before or after it. At one end of the spectrum there are affixes, tiny limpets of grammar which cling on to a word, and change the meaning of it, sometimes utterly, such as '(in)valuable', '(un)necessary', 'posit(ive)' – i.e. making a new, unhyphenated word.

At the other end: simple adverb particles, such as 'off', 'out' and 'up', which can be added on to other words to create phrasal verbs, a constuct with an entirely new purpose – rather like that favourite children's toy, Transformers.

> **76** **Children's or childrens': which is correct and why?**

'Take', for example, means to obtain, receive, even steal something. But add one of our pieces of linguistic Lego and it can represent something entirely different, and what that is varies depending on context. 'Take out', in the mouth of a mafioso, is imbued with homicidal intent, whereas 'takeout' at the pizza parlour suggests the altogether appealing prospect of a meal on the sofa. One can 'check' a fact, but, with add-ons, one goes to a 'check-in' at the air terminal counter and a 'check-out' at a supermarket. In what universe did that happen? One little word changes meaning completely.

77 Are 'inquiry' and 'enquiry' wholly interchangeable?

The wonderful plasticity of language in this respect is one of the little pleasures of the grammar-curious eye. You see it at work everywhere. On the same street you might spot a sign advertising burger and fries at the 'drivethru' before being warned at the gas station that 'driveoffs will be prosecuted'. The additional word brings with it a very specific connotation: 'driveoff' clearly suggests someone attempting to skip out on the petrol charge at the pumps – of course, you are entitled to drive off if you are fully paid up, rather than this being some Sartrean *huis clos* nightmare where one must remain by the pumps for eternity.

> **78** **'Valuable' and 'invaluable'. What's the difference? And why not 'unvaluable'?**

NASA has a little language and grammar of its own which mankind's great step has universalised. Along with the linguistically barbarous 'A-OK', for example, and the logically nonsensical 'failure is not an option', there is a wealth of phrasal verbs, such as 'countdown' (why not 'count-up'?) and, of course, the exultant 'We have lift-off'. It may cross the mind that the simple 'the craft is launched' would be more mellifluous (invoking all those cracked champagne bottles across the bows of vessels). But 'lift-off' (like its close relative in aeronautics, 'take-off') has its own precise, contextual utility. It represents the most fraught moment, when the mass of the rocket and its human cargo (the spam in the can), inertly resisting the thrust of the explosive fuels, is most at risk. This is the moment when 'failure' is not merely an 'option', but a strong possibility.

> **79** **What was the first grammatical error perpetrated on the moon?**

When I was at grammar school, one of the grammatical jests teachers enjoyed making, year in year out, centred on the unfortunate Frenchman (see above, question 20) and his linguistic dilemmas – especially when the ambiguity bred by English phrasal verbs leads to disastrous consequences.

Lets drag our French friend out of the waves and put him on a train. He's still a bit out of it (in both senses, to employ a 'zeugma'), poor fellow.

80   What's a zeugma?

He refreshes himself by leaning out of a carriage window (we're thinking sixties). 'Look out,' you say, 'there's a tunnel coming up.' He looks out and gets his head knocked off. We meant, of course, *retirez votre tête, mon brave, comme la tortue*. But *plus vite*.

He survives. For some exercise we take him into a wood, with an axe, for some recuperative tree felling. Chop that tree down, we say, then chop it up. We come back and find our friend has indeed felled the tree, then painstakingly put it back together again.

There's an (up)side to this English ambiguity. But a (down)side: ambiguity can miscommunicate.

> ### 81
> **You 'fill out' your IRS tax form in the US, 'fill in' your HMRC form in the UK. What odds does it make?**

French, as a few minutes on Google Translate will confirm, is, by nature, not prone to ambiguity (look out! = *attention!* Chop down = *abattre*, chop up = *hacher*). French, manifestly, is much less loose-jointed than English. And its tightness of expression made it, until well into the 20th century, the universal language of diplomacy discourse, where ambiguity can be disastrous. English is now the so-called *lingua franca*. Expect disasters.

Solutions to questions 76–81

76. Children's or childrens': which is correct and why?

Children's is right. A neat explanation is given by 'The English Teacher', on his crofsblogs grammar-for-very-clever-kids website: 'In very old English, we formed plurals not with "s" but with "en": one brother, two brethren; one man, two men; one woman, two women; one child, two children; one chick, two chicken (no kidding!) Some of those words have stayed in the language. They're plurals, but when we form a possessive of them, we treat them as singular: Women's locker room, Children's education'.

77. Are 'inquiry' and 'enquiry' wholly interchangeable?

Usually, but not always. The forthcoming (if it ever comes forth) Goddard 'Inquiry' into historic child abuse will make enquiries among victims. But it will never be referred to as a 'Government Enquiry'.

78. 'Valuable' and 'invaluable'. What's the difference?

The prefix 'in' can sometimes entirely negate the word it is attached to. For example 'capable' and 'incapable' are opposites. In the case of 'valuable' the opposition is more complex. The website grammarist.com sums it up authoritatively: 'Valuable usually applies to things that have monetary value, while invaluable usually applies to things that can't be valued in monetary terms. For example, a hoard of gold is valuable, while a good friend is invaluable.' Oddly, 'valuable' can take the superlative – as in the American sports rating, MVP (Most Valuable Player). 'Most invaluable' feels wrong, although it's occasionally used. One wishes it weren't. A number of privatives are widely used in English today: 'in' (valuable / invaluable), 'a' (syntactic / asyntactic), 'dis', 'mis' (respect / disrespect, spent / misspent), 'im', 'il', 'ir' (immobile, illegal, irremediable), 'non' (speaker / non-speaker) and 'un' (friendly / unfriendly). These negativising affixes, variously of Latin, Greek, German and French origin, sometimes obey their host's etymology, but not invariably. There are also problem cases such as 'flammable' and 'inflammable' which mean exactly the same thing. Most EFL instructors simply give up on rules and tell would-be English speakers to learn the bloody things from a good dictionary and conversation. Cut-and-run grammar.

79. What was the first grammatical error perpetrated on the moon?

Neil Armstrong's 'That's one small step for man, one giant leap for mankind'. He should have said, of course, 'a man'. Armstrong, the most modest of astronauts, later admitted, 'Damn, I really did it. I blew the first words on the moon, didn't I?'

80. What's a zeugma?

Unwarranted yoking – as in 'he's out of the sea and his mind'.

81. You 'fill out' your IRS tax form in the US, 'fill in' your HMRC form in the UK. What odds does it make?

In other circumstances – army commands to men on parade, for example ('fall in!', 'fall out!') – it would matter. What about tax forms? The best answer I've come across is on the English.stack-exchange website, from User15507: 'To me as a German this is very interesting. Seems to me that there must have been some strong influence of German speakers in forming American English. In German you would literally "fill out" a form (*"ein Formular ausfüllen"*). So that might explain the difference between British and American English.' *Danke schön.*

Big words

English usage has been hounded, for the last five centuries, by a pack of Graeco-Latin polysyllables. The orthodoxy was particularly severe – drilled into every well-educated schoolboy – in Browning's day. Some I've personally found useful are below. How many would you, without assistance, know the meaning of?

1. **Pleonasm**

   Verbal upholstery, which adds nothing to the meaning, e.g. 'false pretences', 'future predictions', 'past history'.

2. **Synecdoche** and **metonymy**

   The part standing for the whole, as in 'all hands on deck' or, 'Friends, Romans, Countrymen, lend me your ears'.

3. **Litotes**

   Making molehills out of mountains: as in 'Houston, we have a problem'.

4. **Oxymoron**

   'Military intelligence', 'jumbo shrimp', 'minor miracle'.

5. **Parenthesis**

Interruptive statements placed, usually, in brackets (there are too many in this little book, I've been told).

6. **Tautology**

'This is like déjà vu all over again' (Yogi Berra, baseball player better known as a wit than a slugger).

7. **Anacoluthon**

Sentences which start one way, then go off in an entirely different way, as in the stream of consciousness ending of Joyce's *Ulysses*, when Molly drops off to sleep: 'I put my arms around him yes and drew him down to me so he could feel my breasts all perfume yes and his heart was going like mad and yes I said yes I will Yes.'

8. **Ellipsis**

Dot, dot, dot. Four if there's a sentence break. 'Elliptical' is the derived adjective, representing terse construction. For example Esther's last words about her family in *Bleak House*: 'They can very well do without much beauty in me—even supposing—.'

9. Epistrophe

'It was the best of times. It was the worst of times.' The repetition of that last word rings like a bell. There's also a touch of asyndeton about this opening to *A Tale of Two Cities*, in the omission of the called-for conjunction 'and' or 'but'.

10. Hyperbole

Exaggeration. E.g. 'I'd walk a million miles for one of your smiles.'

This grand terminology is clearly precise and useful. But every time you use one of these terms, or the many, many others, it's like taking a hundred-dollar bill out of your wallet to buy a Big Mac ('false analogy'). Unless you're writing for a learned journal, or playing Scrabble, they are wholly disposable without damage to the goodness of your grammar.

LINGUISTIC HORROR

*T*here have been important advances in language studies in the 20th century. One of the more (mutually) fruitful is a closer relationship with philosophy, particularly in the hybrid known as OLP, 'Ordinary Language Philosophy'. OLP is associated with thinkers such as Wittgenstein and Saussure. The only easy thing about it is its name.

My qualifications, like most of my readers', I suspect, lie elsewhere than philosophy – thinking about thinking. But I find congenial what I take to be Wittgenstein's principle that the use of language in everyday, real-world situations can hit upon meaning and truth.

Wittgenstein's last words on earth were, legend records, 'It's been fun'. 'Fun and games', he might have said, given how 'language games' formed the basis of his philosophy. Games, in their many forms, he explained, are complex human activities. Take chess. It is strictly rule-governed; each piece has its own rules within another rule framework. But within the interlacement created by those rules, an infinite number of different chess games is possible.

There is something very similar in the thinking of the Swiss linguist Ferdinand de Saussure, who made a useful distinction between *langue* (language) and *parole* (any particular speech act).

Langue (language), as Saussure defines it, is like a country – it has finite borders (the population of Somalia, for example, does not speak Polish). But, within its territory, there are infinite routes across. *Parole* refers to any single speech act, within the large terrain of *langue*. These acts will usually be as different as snowflakes – no two ever have the same configuration, while all still being snowflakes.

Within *parole* each of us has what linguists call 'idiolects', our language usages – as much ours as our fingerprints. *Parole* takes liberties, bends and sometimes breaks the rules of *langue*. But the rules are always there. All of us are on parole from the open prison of *langue* when we talk, write, or – insofar as it is verbal – think and dream.

82   What is phatic communication?

The scariest meditation on the use of everyday language, however, is found in the post-Saussurian 'deconstructionist' school of literary-critical theory. The leader of the school, Paul de Man, famously articulated its central theses from an exchange in the TV comedy show, *All in the Family*.

The head of the Bunker family, Archie, is going bowling. His wife, dutifully, laces his shoes. Does he want them laces over or under, she asks. 'What's the difference?' he replies, irritably. 'Doesn't matter,' he means. But, as de Man notes, 'being a reader of sublime simplicity, his wife replies by patiently explaining the difference between lacing over and lacing under'.

De Man ponders this exchange deeply:

> *The confusion can only be cleared up by the interven-*
> *tion of an extra-textual intention, such as Archie Bunker*
> *putting his wife straight; but the very anger he displays is*
> *indicative of more than impatience; it reveals his despair*
> *when confronted with a structure of linguistic meaning*
> *that he cannot control and that holds the discouraging*
> *prospect of an infinity of similar future confusions, all of*
> *them potentially catastrophic in their consequences.*

You might wonder what all this is actually meant to tell us. Well, we exist, as the deconstructionists picture the human condition, on a thin filament over an abyss of meaninglessness. The fragile thread is language. It constantly breaks (deconstructs) and has to be as constantly remade (reconstructed). Grammar is an essential component in the remaking process. The hamster in its wheel has it easy by comparison. But who would want to be a hamster?

Solution to question 82

82. What is phatic communication?

It's 'sociolect', language serving a solely social purpose. It's the verbal equivalent of herd-animals 'flank-rubbing'. The term (it comes from the Greek for 'utterance') was coined by an anthropologist, Bronislaw Malinowski. Silence separates, speech unites. I've noticed, while walking in the San Gabriel mountains in California, that only above 3,000 feet elevation do fellow walkers, on the lonely trail, invariably ask 'how're yadoin?'. They don't want to know; they want a touch of human togetherness. The question is never asked at the trail-head car park. 'How do you do?' is, usually, phatic; no answer is expected. ('Well, since you're kind enough to ask, I have a nasty twinge of rheumatism in my right knee.') Nor is the accompanying handshake intended to reveal (as once it was) that your right hand contains no weapon. We retain the niceties of meaningless language to keep society functioning.

Neurogrammar: Another Kind of Horror

Julianne Moore won a well-deserved 'Best Woman Actor' award at the 2015 Oscars ceremony. One small objection was raised, however, by reviewers.

> 83   'The actor played the part superbly.' What would be the different meanings of this statement in 1615, 1915, and in 2015?

Alzheimer's Disease, which disables Moore's character in the movie, strikes, typically, late in life, when other forms of physical decay are similarly visible. Earlier films (notably *Iris*, about the novelist Iris Murdoch's mental decline) had observed that sad, age-related, fact. Alice Howland, in the 2015 film, is, like the actor who played her, a well-preserved, unwrinkled, professional woman. Hollywood was 'glamorising' – its besetting vice. Or so it was objected.

It could have been avoided if, instead of early-onset Alzheimer's, the scriptwriters had inflicted on Alice frontotemporal dementia (FD). As that grim name indicates, its deteriorative damage to the brain's cells is located, precisely, in the frontal lobes.

FD typically afflicts earlier in life than Alzheimer's. It's usually an inherited condition. 'The age of onset,' one authority observes, 'is typically in the 50s or 60s but can be as young as 30.'

Alice Howland is just 50 years old and a 'rising' professor of linguistics at an Ivy League university, Columbia, with decades of career ahead of her. Until, that is, she becomes, at first mildly, then cata-strophically, 'aphasic'. Loss of control over language is one of the initial warning signs of FD. Specifically symptomatic are errors in grammar: 'a person', we're informed, 'may have "telegraphic speech", habitually leaving out small link words such as "to", "from" or "the"'. The decay of such complex usage is one of the illness's sad milestone markers.

In the film Alice forgets words (first of all the word 'lexicon', ironically enough). Later, gradually and inexorably, her competence erodes, descending at one critical point into the above-described zone of telegraphic speech – her 'grammar' goes. Eventually she becomes completely inarticulate. Filmgoers will probably recall the computer, Hal, in the film *2001: A Space Odyssey* as the hero, Dave, removes its memory banks, one by one. It, too, descends into grammarlessness.

It's tragic, as depicted on screen (for Alice, that is, not the robotically homicidal Hal9000). But what Moore's sensitively observed depiction alerts us to is the fact that there is, it would seem, a part of our brain that is specifically dedicated to grammar. We are, it's fair to assume, 'wired' for grammar. *Homo sapiens* is *Homo grammaticus*. When the brilliant theoretical linguist Noam Chomsky introduced this idea – that grammar is innate, inborn – it was controversial. Now, half a century later, an organic element in language acquisition is generally accepted, but how it operates is hotly disputed.

Solution to question 83

83. 'The actor played the part superbly.' What would be the different meanings of this statement in 1615, 1915, and in 2015?

In 1615, it would denote any actor, but they could be only a man or boy. Women were not allowed to play on the professional stage until later in the century, when the French word *actrice* was anglicised as 'actress' to categorise them as female. The feminine versions of other words of Latin origin are formed in a similar way: inheritrix, victrix, and – later in history – aviatrix. In 1915, the term 'actor' denoted a male performer, exclusive of the female contingent of the profession. In 2015, actor was widely, but not entirely, gender-neutralised to refer to a man or woman. It was well meaning but messy. In a debate on the Stage website it was pointed out that the conundrum statement 'Helen Mirren is the finest actor of her age' would not make clear whether she was better than all other performers, or just the females. The word's gender–neutrality can also cause a trans-sex confusion in the statement: 'The actor played the heroine brilliantly.' (Is Shakespeare's Cleopatra, by the way, a 'hero'?) Speaking for myself, I'd rather like to hear over the intercom, in a female voice: 'Welcome to Progressive Airlines, ladies and gentlemen. This is your *aviatrix* speaking...'

Reflections in a verbal graveyard

Like their speakers, words are born, copulate, breed and die. Some, among the dead, have served whatever purpose they ever had and are best gone. Of others we may regret the passing. Here are ten I, personally, would like exhumed. How many of them are lodged in your vocabulary?

1. Phrontistery

A thinking-place; place for study. The *OED* tracks it back to 1623, adding, 'Formerly freq. used with allusion to Aristophanes' representation of the school of Socrates; hence sometimes ironically.' Not entirely helpful.

2. Incarnadine

The word is used, famously, by Lady Macbeth, looking at her (forever) blood-stained hands: 'This my Hand will rather / The multitudinous Seas incarnadine, / Making the Green one Red.' The *OED* notes it was formerly used neutrally, meaning 'to redden'. Shakespeare infused it, permanently, with overtones of blood and it fell out of general use.

3. **Widdershins**

It means 'arse about face'. As useful, in horizontal description, as 'topsy-turvy' is in vertical description.

4. **Pilcrow**

This should be in the punctuational questionnaire. A paragraph mark, as old as the history of printing itself. It's revived in SGML, Standard General Markup Language (for computers) as the tag '<p>'.

5. **Swive**

A word all students of Chaucer know. As the *OED* prissily glosses it, 'To have sexual connection with, copulate with (a female)'.

6. **Twat**

As the *OED* says, a low term for the vagina, adding, 'Erroneously used (after quot. 1660) by Browning *Pippa Passes* iv. ii. 96 under the impression that it denoted some part of a nun's attire.' Useful because it has been decontaminated as a usable C-word. 'Twattish behaviour' is, for example, wholly inoffensive (198 hits on the *Guardian*, for example, and none of them letters of complaint).

7. **Pell-mell**

In a disorganised crowd. Jumbled up. It survives as a street name for that most crowded of London thoroughfares, on royal occasions, Pall Mall.

8. **Yelve**

Dung fork. Strictly speaking, we can get by without this noun of Anglo-Saxon parentage, coming, as it does, from a period when sewage needed more than a toilet handle. Oddly, though, the word has an afterlife as 'gavel' – the kind of pseudo-dung fork a judge bangs for order in court.

9. **Sprunt**

Mark Forsyth, in an article on 'Lost Words' in the *Guardian* (9 October 2013) laments its disappearance. It's 'an old Scots word (from Roxburgh, to be precise)', he tells us, 'meaning "to chase girls around among the haystacks after dark".' A-sprunting we will go.

10. **Kench**

Used in Middle English, meaning 'to bellow with laughter'. 'Belly-laugh' has that origin, but somehow doesn't work. Kench would be preferable. May it live again.

I could go on, but not, alas, in a short book. Enough to say, with Eliot and Dante, 'I had not thought death had undone so many [words].' For a delightful ramble through this wild-wordy territory see Mark Forsyth's 2011 bestseller, *The Etymologicon*.

CONTEXT: SITUATIONAL GRAMMAR

I've put this at the end because it makes the point I'd most like to stress – namely the defining power of situation, what grammarians call 'context'.

Context, or situationality, is easily demonstrated and one negotiates it many times a day. At the level of phrasal semantics, a 'hat-trick' is a very different thing if performed by a bowler with a cricket ball, or a magician on stage, pulling rabbits from his topper. 'A titter ran round the court' has much ruder connotations when lewdly said by Frankie Howerd on the Palladium stage than it does when written in *The Times* by their senior court reporter, fearful of a 'contempt of court offence' (i.e. laughing at judges).

Circumstance makes meaning. 'Take off', to revisit the linguistic lego discussion, means something different on an airport runway from what it means when an impressionist 'takes off' (i.e. impersonates) some public figure. And different again when a stripper renders her scanty coverings scantier. 'All change' means different, instantly comprehensible things in (1) a railway station and (2) a dressing room.

Time (temporal situation), like scenario (spatial situation), remoulds meaning and usage round past or current circumstance. The word 'historic', for example, is used primarily to mean, as any Oxford dictionary will tell you, something 'glorious'. Nelson won a historic ('an' historic?) victory at Trafalgar.

---

84   What do 'synchronic' and 'diachronic' mean?

Police jargon, in the period after the Jimmy Savile revelations, began applying 'historic', in their public announcements, to criminal sexual acts perpetrated in the distant past. They should have said 'historical'. Rolf Harris and Max Clifford were convicted of what were described as 'historic sex crimes'. It did not imply anything glorious. 'Historic' is now, thanks to institutional misuse, a filth-encrusted adjective. It brings a bad smell with it. The word is probably beyond fumigation for a generation or two.

---

85   What's the difference between 'imply' and 'infer'?

The circumstantial change wrought by time is one of the things which make literary criticism (discussion, typically, of old writing by long dead people) fun. Or funny. Groucho Marx always got a laugh by saying, instead of 'it cost me a packet', 'I disbursed a goodly sum'.

The power of historical circumstance is clearly inscribed on the reputational history of one of the perennially censored (yet loved) literary texts in the US – *Huckleberry Finn*. Currently Mark Twain's story offends because of its profligate use of the N-word (which appears nineteen times). A purified 'teaching' edition was produced in 2011 in which the offending vocable, and its compounds, were replaced with 'slave'. Well meaning, of course; but somehow the purged text doesn't ring true; any more than would Rhett Butler saying, 'Frankly, my dear, I don't give a darn' (which is what many high-ups at MGM wanted Gable to say).

When it first came out, Twain's book was criticised and banned, by educators and librarians, not for its 'racist' word (no such offence in the 19th century) but for its bad grammar. For example, the first sentence:

> *You don't know about me without you have read a book by the name of* The Adventures of Tom Sawyer; *but that ain't no matter.*

The Concord Public Library in Massachusetts issued a papal condemnation of Huck's memoir when the book first came out:

> *it deals with a series of adventures of a very low grade of morality; it is couched in the language of a rough dialect, and all through its pages there is a systematic use of bad grammar and an employment of rough, coarse, inelegant expressions.*

Precisely. The point cleverer Mr Twain was making was that 'dialects' – the 'little languages' of small places with their own rules – have their own idioms, vocabulary and idiosyncratic grammars. These have local validity, and their zones of deviation create a cultural community. Twain posts a warning at the head of his story:

> *In this book a number of dialects are used, to wit: the Missouri negro dialect; the extremest form of the back-woods Southwestern dialect; the ordinary 'Pike County' dialect; and four modified varieties of this last. The shadings have not been done in a haphazard fashion, or by guesswork; but painstakingly, and with the trustworthy guidance and support of personal familiarity with these several forms of speech.*

Dialectally, and within his linguistic region, Huck's classroom incorrectness is correct. Zonally. For readers outside the zone, he is everything the Concord librarians say he is. The librarians' point is that loose grammar means loose morals. Every Widow Douglas in history would agree with them.

Mark Twain didn't. Nor do I.

Solutions to questions 84–85

84. What do 'synchronic' and 'diachronic' mean?

Literally what's going on now, and what used to go on in language in the past. Nowadays (synchronically) it would be quaintly antique to say 'I disbursed a goodly sum'. But (diachronically) 'It cost me an arm and a leg' would be meaningless to a Victorian. 'This was the most unkindest cut of all,' says Mark Antony in *Julius Caesar*. None of the groundlings in the Globe, one can be sure, shuddered at the double superlative – which drives a tank through the Fowler *King's English* lawn. (What's that I see over there in the bushes? Kingsley Amis with a bazooka?) Synchronically, in its own time, 'most unkindest cut' was perfectly good grammar, rules being very elastic in Shakespeare's day.

85. What's the difference between 'imply' and 'infer'?

There's a nice explanation on the livewritethrive website: 'You imply things through your own words. You infer things from someone else's words.' Nuff said.

86   'The poor saps condemned to labour in this environment – deliberately designed so the bosses can see whether any galley slaves are doing something unproductive like talking to another human being – soon learn to fear the very place designed for them to interact in.' Jeremy Paxman, in the *Guardian*, August 2014, on the iniquities of open-plan offices. What's Paxo's grammatical error?

87   Someone walks into a door you carelessly left ajar and hurts themself. 'I'm sorry,' you say. It can mean two different things, or both at the same time: (1) **'I'm sorry I left the door open.'** (2) **'I'm sorry you're hurt.'** Assuming you mean one rather than the other, how, in the anxiety of the moment could you, without wasting words, indicate which of the two you mean?

88   **The suffix '-ed'**, in the past-tenses of verbs, is one
      of the many minefields for those setting out to
      learn spoken English. How, for example, would
      a native speaker pronounce 'I determined...'
      ('determinD'), 'I defended...' ('defendED'),
      'I passed by' ('pasT'). Is there any grammatical
      rule that helps?

89   In his summing up, in November 2012, Lord
      Leveson, passing his scathing verdict on
      the British Press's phone-tapping practices,
      declared it had **'wreaked havoc in the lives
      of innocent people for many decades'**. Why
      does 'wreaked' grate on the ears of those of
      refined grammatical sensibility, and is there a
      preferable form of the word?

90   I bought the computer I'm currently using in the
      US, and my auto-correct automatically alters
      my '-ise' ending words (e.g. recognise) to '-ize'
      (recognize). So be it. **But why do I get irri-
      tated at 'analyze'?**

91   Is there any reason for retaining the Britishism
      'amongst', when **'among'** serves equally well?
      Or does it?

92   'Rise in Child and Teen Fraud Arrests Mainly Due to Increase of Internet-based Crimes', headline in the *Daily Telegraph*, 12 April 2015. Should it be 'owing to Increase…'?

93   The following sentence is found in the *New York Times*, 15 March 2015, in a report about Ellen Pao's suit against her Wall Street employers, on grounds of gender discrimination ('them' refers to junior males in the firm): **'Not surprisingly, none of them are willing to discuss their experience on the record because they fear the consequences to their careers.'** Overlooking the awful start to this sentence, should it be 'none of them is…'?

94   **'So take a moment / To wonder why / The world keeps turning / For you and I.'** From 10cc's top-selling track, 'For You and I'. What's the error?

95   This is one of the most famous openings in English poetry: **'Of man's first disobedience, and the fruit / Of that forbidden tree, whose mortal taste / Brought death into the world, and all our woe, / With loss of Eden, till one greater man / Restore us, and regain**

the blissful seat, /Sing heavenly muse.' Why does not, as normal English practice would demand, 'Sing heavenly muse…' come as the first, rather than the last, clause in the sentence? As Yoda would say, 'Wrong it seems. A reason must there be'. What's the reason?

96 Front-page headline, *London Evening Standard*, 17 March 2015: **'Judges Axed for Looking at Porn in Office'**. What's wrong, if anything, with the sentence?

97 The most famous line in Stephen Spender's poetry, routinely quoted in great men's (or is it mens'?) funerals – President Kennedy's, for example – is **'I think continually of those who were truly great'**. It's routinely misquoted as 'I think continuously…' Why is that wrong? Or is it?

98 Headline in *The Times*, 14 March 2015: **'Cameron Demands Inquiry into Spy Snooping on Calls and Texts'**. What's objectionable?

99 My answer to the above question utilises the phrase: **'such as Assange, or Snowden…'**

I thought of writing **'like Assange and Snowden'**, but didn't. Why?

100   *Irregardless* – the title of Australian Felicity Ward's stand-up comedy act. Ungrammatical or what?

Solutions to questions 86–100

86. 'The poor saps condemned to labour in this environment [...] soon learn to fear the very place designed for them to interact in.' What's Paxo's grammatical error?

Paxman's long, shoddy sentence ends in a preposition – the word 'in' (i.e. denoting placement). *Pre*position means just that – it should come *before*, not be '*post*positioned' *after* other items in the sentence. Or so grammar purists insist. There are, however, more liberal authorities who go along with what is called 'preposition stranding'. Subtextually what Paxman's imperfect sentence intimates is 'I'm so pissed off, screw the grammar'. Accompanied, of course, by that famous paint-stripper glare.

87. (1) 'I'm sorry I left the door open.' (2) 'I'm sorry you're hurt.' How do you indicate which one you mean?

I'd suggest if (1) the single word 'Sorry!' and if (2) the addition of a sympathetic, pain-sharing, exclamative, 'Ouch! I'm sorry!' Most of us solve the problem intuitively. Or don't. Not really a question, merely wondering. It happened to me this morning. NB Use of 'themself' in the question — ugly, but a necessary terminological vagueness, if the gender of the subject is not identified.

88. The suffix '-ed'. How would a native speaker pronounce 'I determined' ('determinD'), 'I defended' ('defendED'), 'I passed by' ('pasT')? Is there any grammatical rule that helps?

No. As Professor Aarts tells me, it is a matter of phonology and conventional usages, not grammar.

89. The Press were said to have 'wreaked havoc in the lives of innocent people for many decades'. Why does 'wreaked' grate, and is there a preferable form of the word?

Yes. There is a group of 70-odd so-called 'strong' verbs whose past tense remains atavistically Middle English; 'brought', not 'bringed', 'bought' not 'buyed', for example. Until recently 'wreak'

168

/ 'wrought' was one of them. But strong verbs are an endangered linguistic species and recently 'wreaked havoc' (the most common phrasal usage) has replaced 'wrought havoc', which sounds sweeter to my ear. As does 'fraught' for the past tense of 'freaked' (though no one uses it). Snuck (sneaked) and dove (dived) I can live without, although Americans can't.

90. Why do I get irritated at 'analyze'?

I'm with Fowler on this: 'Analyse is better than analyze, but merely as being the one of the two equally indefensible forms that has won. The correct but now impossible form would be analysize (or analysise), with analysist for existing analyst.'

91. Why retain 'amongst', when 'among' serves equally well. Or does it?

Generally, yes. But Fowler makes a slight plea for retention: 'Few perhaps would say amongst strangers with among to hand, amongst us is easier to say than among us.' Ease of saying is not a bad reason. We have 'length, breadth, width', then why not the once legitimate 'heighth'? Because it's so difficult to say in a hurry.

92. 'Rise in Child and Teen Fraud Arrests Mainly Due to Increase of Internet-based Crimes.' Should it be 'owing to Increase...'?

It's a notoriously foggy area of grammar, but the *Telegraph* is probably in grammatical error. Then again, it's one of those 'who cares?' things. Go ahead and be care-less.

93. 'None of them are willing to discuss their experience on the record.' Should it be 'none of them is...'?

According to Fowler most certainly yes. Could you say 'No one of them are...'? But that noise you hear is Fowler, spinning in his grave, his 'rule' alongside him. It's gone by the board. And none of us is / are / ain't sorry to see the pesky quibble go.

94. 'So take a moment / To wonder why / The world keeps turning / For you and I.' What's the error?

It hits you in the eye, so to speak. 'For', as in Latin, takes the accusative. It should be 'For You and Me'. To illustrate the point with an earlier top-selling song, how would 'The bells are ringing, for I and my girl' sound? 'Between you and I' is a more common misusage, nowadays, but still grating to the grammar-sensitive ear.

95. Of man's first disobedience, and the fruit / Of that forbidden tree […] Sing heavenly muse.' Why doesn't 'Sing heavenly muse…' come as the first clause?

Milton first wanted to write what became *Paradise Lost* in Latin. Then, when he decided to 'English' the poem, he resolved to raise his crude material by utilising overtly Latinate devices such as this suspension – postponing the verb, requiring the reader, like a juggler, to keep the foregoing sense unfixed in the mind. Germans, whose language routinely suspends the verb to the end of the statement, claim it makes their language more fit for philosophy, because the mind has to hold what is being said more firmly in place (*weil der Geist muss halten, was man mehr fest an seinem Platz, sagte*). As an extra bonus, it allowed Milton to get 'disobedience' – which is what the poem is all about – in at the beginning.

96. 'Judges Axed for Looking at Porn in Office.' What's wrong – if anything?

'In Office' could mean while enjoying bewigged and gowned judicial rank ('all stand'), or getting a clandestine look on their chambers' computer ('John Thomas. Stand!'). Or both. Headline compositors, with a lot to say, and little space to say it, are cunning compressors / combiners. I suspect the suppressed zeugma ('yoking' of two meanings) was deliberate.

97. 'I think continually of those who were truly great' is routinely misquoted as 'I think continuously...' Why is that wrong? Or is it?

It's wrong. 'Continuously' would suggest he never stopped thinking about it and thought about very little else. As Spender's biographer, I can vouch for the fact that he often thought about other things. Money, for example.

98. 'Cameron Demands Inquiry into Spy Snooping on Calls and Texts.' What's objectionable?

General looseness, specifically an undefined nominative. It could, to the thoughtless eye, be thought that the PM wants to haul some individual 'snooper', such as Assange, or Snowden, over the coals. What is meant, of course, is widespread, institutional espionage, as at GCHQ. That snarling you hear is Lynne Truss. A hyphen ('Spy-Snooping') would solve the problem but headline writers hate hyphens.

99. 'Such as Assange, or Snowden...' not 'like Assange and Snowden'. Why?

'Such as' is more dignified-sounding – 'like' having been besmirched ('beshitten', as our resident Middle-English-Man would say) by its use as, like, just sentence putty, like, by young, like, speakers.

There is another small but valid reason for the choice suggested by Grammar Girl: '"like" implies comparison; "such as" implies inclusion.' Can you imagine 'the Greatest' saying 'I float such as a bird do, I sting such as a bee do'? There's more of an 'along with' in the Snowden / Assange sentence, I think, warranting 'such as'. If I'd written 'Snowden or Assange', 'like' would have been preferable. Like it matters.

100. *Irregardless* – ungrammatical or what?

For some reason this is a lapse in grammar that makes Grammar Nazis reach for their Lugers. The prefix is, of course, redundant. Who would say 'Carry on Irregardless', rather than 'regardless'? Its main attraction, though, is that the extra syllable gives you time to think how to end the sentence, which can be, 'err, err, errregardless', useful on occasion. 'Hesitation phenomena', they're called.

WHITHER GRAMMAR

Where is grammar going? There is little one can confidently say. In the short term – every generation or so – it will be subject to battles about 'good' (i.e. disciplinary) grammar and liberationist grammar. That can be expected.

In the longer term, much will depend on the Rumsfeldian known-unknowns – future technology, national and geopolitical shifts, politics, class changes, war, peace, immigration, generational conflict. The list is very long and the interactions incalculable. One might as well trace the flight paths of mayflies.

But, not to play the prophet, I see possible directions and intertwinings. One is more machine language, adapted, like primal 140-character text, to new communication technologies. This, probably, will be more pictographic and sonorous. Language with its own sound track.

But, coming from where I do, culturally, I would

like to think that the richness of language, built up over millennia, will be preserved and enhanced by – what else? – poetry, in its larger, Platonic sense of 'literature', constantly renewing the language of the tribe. One can end with the life- and language-affirming words of Matthew Arnold:

> *The future of poetry is immense, because in poetry, where it is worthy of its high destinies, our race, as time goes on, will find an ever surer and surer stay.*

Language too.

Acknowledgments

Everyone who lives by the pen should have a grammar guide as well as a dictionary always within reach. The helpmate I would recommend is *The Oxford Modern English Grammar* by Bas Aarts; a distillation of UCL/SEU thinking and practice. Much of what is discussed here (Mr Gove's views on grammar, for example) is dealt with, wittily and as quick response in Professor Aarts's blog, *Grammarianism*.[3]

'Grammar Nerds', as they call themselves, are a sharing community. As is evident, I have gratefully borrowed from their blogged wit, wisdom and occasional crankiness. More details are in the Further Reading section. I thank Bas Aarts for looking over what I've written and Paul Bougourd for his tactfully expert editorial supervision. Errors and other objectionable things are wholly mine.

---

3 For the entry on Gove, see: https://grammarianism.wordpress.com/2015/06/22/however/

Further Reading

In its upper academic reaches the study of grammar is as technically demanding as the study of physics. Those who know that fact will need no advice on reading from me. Those merely curious about the current scholarly tier of grammatical research will get a taste in Professor Bas Aarts's foregoing 'Some everyday phrases put through the grammatical wringer' (p.78).

Also commended as a good starting point for the curious is *The Oxford Dictionary of English Grammar* by Bas Aarts, Sylvia Chalker and Edmund Weiner (OUP second edn, 2014).

The biblical study of language which emerged, after decades of work, from the Survey of English Usage unit which Professor Aarts now heads, is *A Comprehensive Grammar of the English Language* by Randolph Quirk, Sidney Greenbaum, Geoffrey Leech and Geoffrey Jan Svartvik (Longman, 1985).

Unlike physics, all of us use language and grammar

every minute of every day of our lives, in thought, expression and communication. Insofar as language comes into our dreams, grammar also inhabits our unconscious nights as well. We live in grammar as vitally as we live in the air we breathe. Without it we would be nothing.

Because it is so essential to what we are, as human beings, there is constantly bubbling commentary on, and dispute about, language and grammar. We're all experts – we talk and write don't we?

This discussion is fascinating and – for the thinking person – a source of fun. We can enjoy, even if we do not choose to kiss the rod and obey, the disciplinary strictures of Henry Watson Fowler and his grumpy disciple Kingsley Amis: *Fowler's Modern English Usage* (OUP new edn, 2002); *The King's English* (Penguin Classics, with an Introduction by Martin Amis, 2011).

We can certainly read for pleasure and instruction, coated with wit, the recent crop of popular dissertations on the subject, for example (to cite those which I have profited from, and been entertained by): N. M. Gwynne, *Gwynne's Grammar* (Tradibooks, 2012); Simon Heffer, *Strictly English: The Correct Way to Write... and Why it Matters* (Random House, 2010); Oliver Kamm, *Accidence Will Happen: The Non-Pedantic Guide to English Usage* (Weidenfeld and Nicolson, 2015); Harry

Ritchie, *English for the Natives: Discover the Grammar You Don't Know You Know* (John Murray, 2013); Lynne Truss, *Eats, Shoots & Leaves* (Profile, 2003).

There are many grammar blogs. I have been most entertainingly instructed by Grammar Girl's 'Quick and Dirty Tips'. Others are referenced elsewhere in the foregoing text.

One last word: enjoy.

Index of Grammatical Terms

John Sutherland – Lord Northcliffe
Professor Emeritus, UCL – is the author
of over 30 works of scholarship and writes,
regularly, for the London and New York
Times, the London *Guardian* and many
places else (spot the solecism).